Steele!

With appreciation

& love.

May you always be

surrounded by beauty &

lifted with great joy.

Cheers!

Love

ENTERTAINING
by DESIGN

A Guide to Creating Meaningful Gatherings

LORNA GROSS

PHOTOGRAPHY BY ROBERT RADIFERA
AND KEYANNA BOWEN

THE
collective
BOOK STUDIO

For Autumn and Blake, two of my greatest inspirations.
May you continue to soar, be relentless in pursuing your dreams,
and remember to always follow the Light that surrounds you and the
Light that is within you.

All my love, LoLo

To Marie and Cleadine, two strong, trailblazing women
I never had the pleasure of meeting but who inspired this book and
propelled me to stay the course.

contents

in interior design and after opening my firm, I've been fulfilling the aesthetic dreams for clientele around the world for more than eighteen years. My success has been primarily attributed to my love affair with uniqueness, my huge affinity for statement pieces, and my heightened appreciation of human connection.

I am also that party hostess and planner who believes every gathering should be an experience that the attendees will find hard to forget. Not simply because of the food or the aesthetics but because they sensed that Love was present through the care applied to the execution and the way they felt valued in each moment they spent.

Out of those experiences, philosophies, and my unrelenting passion for food and its presentation, I am sharing some stories about my most memorable occasions around food and well-designed gatherings. And I will demonstrate to you how to pull it all together. If you're reading this book, you are likely someone who also appreciates the joys that fellowship can offer.

In a time when our lives are super busy and we don't have the bandwidth to create hand-crafted table décor or plan a supersonic soirée, it often feels like a huge task to pull together a brunch, formal dinner, casual gathering, or intimate party without becoming completely overwhelmed.

In these pages, I reveal some manageable recommendations for the ideal ways to go about creating gatherings that are both memorable and beautiful—and without needing a year-long vacation once it's done. Since I'm a type A, business-owner, and mother, sometimes I have to save myself from myself and take the *easy road*. With that in mind, I've also offered some shortcuts and time-saving suggestions on how to make a big impact with a lot less work.

The best gatherings engage as many senses as possible. So, from interesting tablescapes to divine recipes to musical vibes, join me on a journey through a series of year-round occasions—some special and some just simple and relaxed.

Let's indulge in a palette of décor, food, beauty, and fellowship.

ESSENTIAL ELEMENTS FOR THE TABLETOP

Any gathering around food requires some essential items. You may not need all of them, but having the basics on hand or at least on your "must have" list will go a long way in saving you time and energy when you are planning a party. Having these essentials stored and ready to use can alleviate stress and make planning so much easier because you can focus most of your attention on the perishable items that can only be purchased close to the event date.

Dinner Plates I know this sounds boring, but nothing beats a set of white dinner plates. If you entertain a lot for casual and formal occasions, invest in both a casual set and a more elegant set—maybe with a metallic rim of gold or silver to add a bit of glam to your tabletop. I prefer purchasing in multiples of four, like eight or twelve, but you can decide the number that works best for you. This basic set can be used for almost any type of party.

Accent Plates and Bowls If your style is uber contemporary, you can purchase simple white salad or dessert plates. These plates will also give you an opportunity to add a bit of character to your table setting. If you're really into it, you can purchase a few sets of these in hues that harken to the season of the year or the holiday you may be celebrating. I love that they can add a punch of color or artistry to the tabletop. You can also opt to complete your set with bowls if you like to serve soup or stews. They can also be used for serving.

Drinking Glasses Having glasses on hand that can hold six to eight ounces of liquid are ideal to accommodate water, iced tea, lemonade, or any other favorite refreshment.

Wineglasses Stemmed wineglasses are easier to knock over than stemless, but they add varying height to the tabletop, which gives it a nice three-dimensionality. These glasses can be used for wine or non-alcoholic sparkling cider.

Colored Glasses From soft neutrals to pastels to deep, rich pigments, colored glasses can help convey the mood you're creating with your tabletop. They can communicate anything from a gentle, fresh feeling to a sensual, dramatic vibe, depending on what you're trying to achieve.

Casual Flatware If you entertain primarily in a more low-key fashion, a set of simple, everyday flatware will do. Essential components for a casual place setting include, from left to right, a salad fork, a dinner fork, a dinner knife, and a soup spoon. (See page 241 for information on setting the table.)

Formal Flatware If you also entertain more formally, you may want to add a teaspoon and maybe a dessert spoon or fork.

Dinner Napkins Simple white or off-white cloth dinner napkins are always a nice touch on the tabletop. You can purchase some with a little embroidery detail or dress them up with decorative rings that relate to the occasion.

Cocktail Napkins These are smaller napkins that are great for drinks or appetizers.

Blooms and Botanicals There is a richness and sense of beauty and life that flowers or green foliage add to a tabletop. Depending on the kind you prefer, they can also be used to reinforce the mood you're setting for your gathering. (See page 238 for more information on flowers.)

Vases It's nice to have on hand a few vases in varying sizes and heights. Not only will they hold your flowers and greenery, but they will also contribute to the style and mood of your event along with all the other elements on the table. Taller, more narrow, and shorter vases can also help keep flowers from blocking the view of diners across the table, which will enable everyone to converse with the group.

Candles If you enjoy entertaining in the evening, consider incorporating candles. They can create the most beautiful ambience and elevate the appearance and feel of your occasion. (See page 240 for more information on candles.)

OPPOSITE, CLOCKWISE FROM TOP LEFT: Napkins can be dressed up with interesting napkin rings or ties, which adds drama and texture. Tall flowers like snapdragons make a dramatic statement and can be a focal point to your table. Elevate any gathering with unique glassware.

Platters They say presentation is everything, and I totally agree. The way you serve your favorite dish matters in how guests perceive it. Selecting a few integral serving pieces can go a long way. Begin with foundational components, including a platter for meat, poultry, or fish; a vegetable dish; and a casserole dish.

Serving Bowls Try to have a few different sizes and styles of serving bowls available. These are really useful for a wide range of foods and can also be used to decorate a table—pile a few glass holiday ornaments in a serving bowl and you'll have a lovely focal point. I like using beautiful casserole dishes that can go from the oven to the table.

Specialty Serving Dishes Sometimes it's nice to have additional serving pieces such as gravy boats, a sauce server, a sugar bowl and creamer, or condiment bowls. They certainly aren't mandatory, but they can be useful as well as add elegance to the table, especially if they are part of your dinnerware set, or they can add quirkiness by using contrasting antique or whimsical pieces.

Serving Utensils Don't forget that you will need utensils to serve the food. Look for salad fork and spoon sets, large serving spoons, attractive tongs, and pie and cake servers.

BELOW: Decorating with botanicals like these brilliant green ferns offers pops of contrasting color.

Salt and Pepper Shakers One way to add something unexpected to your tabletop is by utilizing decorative salt and pepper shakers or dispensers. They can make a dramatic statement, create elegance, or add a pop of fun.

Place Cards Having name cards or folded tent cards on hand is a great way to make things easy and personal for your guests when it's time to sit down for the meal. In design, we use a term called "wayfinding." This is when signage is used to help people find their way. Place cards can assist people in finding their seat, identify what kind of food is in a dish, or mark an occasion with a slogan. They make things easier for your guests, and you as the host will have fewer questions to answer.

Card Holders Place card holders can be found in a variety of designs and can coordinate to the theme of the occasion, such as ones with floral accents for spring, woven materials for outdoor dining, or ornaments for the holiday season. Although small, they can add a lovely accent to the tabletop in addition to serving the functional purpose of marking the name of a person or dish.

I often use small picture frames at buffets to designate items on the menu, ingredients, or special instructions.

ABOVE, LEFT: Reusable place cards allow you to label the different foods you might be serving or personalize a place setting. **ABOVE, RIGHT:** Serving utensils, like these gold-toned cheese knives make great accent pieces.

~ spring ~

What is it about springtime that ushers in joy and the hope of beautiful things to come? To me, everything about the season is hopeful. Dogwoods and cherry trees blossom, tulips and daffodils start to bloom—even the rain showers help motivate seedlings to sprout. Suddenly what appeared dead is now renewed. It only stands to reason that this is the most perfect time to gather together to celebrate life and the promise of wonderful things on the horizon.

In springtime, color returns to greet us with magnificence. Botanicals and fruit in yellows, reds, oranges, and greens all convey so much joy that we didn't even realize we were thirsty for. And who doesn't love brilliant yellow daffodils and other spring flowers like tulips and lilies? These gorgeous blooms make it easy to shrug off those winter blues.

There's so much to celebrate—Easter, Passover, Eid, Mother's Day, Graduations, Memorial Day, Father's Day, and Juneteenth. And if you live in a warmer climate, this is also when art and music festivals launch. There are so many reasons to gather, and if this list doesn't do it for you, come together with friends and family just because. After a long and sometimes isolating winter, spring is when people are longing to reconnect. So, let's gather together and do just that!

Once, I was asked by an overly protective family member, "Why do you always have to be the one to host?" At this moment, I'm trying to remember if I ever responded—which is probably not the best way to answer a question. But I do know that the answer is that I love food and I love bringing people together, so I really should have said, "Why not?" If you're also someone who needs no excuse to gather folks together, hop on this buffet dinner train with me.

I'm told that my great-grandmother (for whom I carry my middle name, Marie) used to host dinners and celebrations at her house in Brooklyn, New York, back in the 1940s and '50s. She was a church minister, quite remarkable for a woman of her time. It is said that when she was a child she died and came back to life and ever since she was thought to have supernatural powers. She used some of those to invite over family members and folks from the church and the neighborhood for some good eats on a regular basis. Feeding people was her thing, and she was known for bringing the community together around a great meal. So, I guess I come by this hosting thing naturally. Those superpowers are in my genes.

Okay, let's just admit that one of the best features of a buffet dinner is that it is an *all-you-can-eat* smorgasbord of goodies. I mean, who doesn't want to have the license to keep coming back for more of their favorite items on the menu? This setting actually encourages you to stuff your belly with tasty morsels until you're about to burst. How many opportunities in life do we get like that? Honestly, if it's a buffet dinner, count me in.

The key to a great one is to keep a casual approach and make it easy for your guests. When I set this up, I like to display all the options on the kitchen island or on a credenza so hungry guests can prowl around for a moment or two before they seek out their prey. Stack the plates or set them up in baskets to begin. The most essential décor item of the buffet dinner is the name cards that help guests identify each dish. Use little tented cards or place the cards in cute picture frames to get the job done. If you know you'll have vegetarians or guests with food allergies attending, it's nice to list the critical ingredients or mark them as gluten-free or vegan-friendly. This actually helps you enjoy

the gathering more because your guests don't have to come to you to ask whether the jambalaya has chicken or pork in it.

And speaking of jambalaya, being able to keep these kinds of dishes warm or on display in a slow cooker is another essential. (And can we all agree that the inventor of the slow cooker was a genius?) Besides offering one or two homemade dishes, I often opt to supplement the meal with catered food or high-end grocery store prepared sides and desserts to save time and make my job easier.

Lastly, if you choose to utilize a kitchen island or peninsula, feel free to lay a folded tablecloth or a table throw over the countertop to dress up the display a bit. Cutting boards over stove tops or sinks also help unify the appearance and provide additional serving space. Tall statuesque flowers add a touch of elegance and can help distract the eye from cabinetry and harsher-appearing appliances. Placing pretty green leaves like ferns around the dishes softens the surroundings and makes a big impact without a lot of extra effort.

OPPOSITE AND ABOVE: Use serving dishes and plates at different heights to create interest and dimension on your tabletop.

Prosciutto
Panino

Fin
Po

MOODY FORMAL DINNER

Carpe diem! Why not seize the day and cultivate new relationships in this season of fresh beginnings? After nesting for months at home during what often feels like cold, dreary times, people are ready to venture out into the world again. Go ahead and invite over some folks from work, some kindred spirits from a charity organization that you support, or a couple of parents from your kids' school. Ask yourself the question: Who would I like to get to know a little better? Or flip that—Who would I like to get to know me a little better?

Now you have the perfect guests for a formal dinner. The secret sauce is that if you have a friend or two who is always good for keeping the conversation going, invite them too.

My childhood was filled with formal table settings. Every Sunday evening my sister, Sharon, and I would be responsible for setting the table for our family of four in the dining room. Once in a while, additional family or friends would attend, but mostly it was just us. This was my first introduction to how beautiful a set table can make a person feel. There is an elevated sense of elegance that occurs when you eat at a gorgeous place setting. Let's be honest, even store-bought potpies served on beautiful china taste like a gourmet meal.

The formal dinner is best executed around a fully set table that is elegant and sophisticated. Your guests will immediately feel special when they take in the beauty before them. Flowers, like orchids, instantly conjure a more refined ambience, and because they're not overly leafy they won't obstruct the view across the table.

Set the arrival time for guests to about a half hour prior to serving dinner so you can be sure that your guests are all present when it's time to eat. If you can, before they are seated, gather them in a separate space where you might have soft music and a little wine and cheese set out for them while they wait.

ABOVE, CLOCKWISE FROM TOP LEFT: Orchids are great for a formal table. Little details, like the adorable turtle salt and pepper shakers can be conversation starters. A formal party is the time to bring out the special china.

By the way, the most essential décor item for an exceptional formal dinner is the place card—especially if you're hosting a meal with strangers. Where you seat your guests matters, because you want everyone to meet each other and converse freely. If those who already know each other are all clustered together, the new folks could feel left out. These name cards don't have to be formally printed (that's too much work for me). I just write them neatly by hand.

One of my go-tos for a formal dinner with strangers is to write little notes or words on the back of place cards that reference little-known fun facts (something I think they'll enjoy learning) about the people sitting next to them. They are useful icebreakers to get the conversation started.

If done well, by the end of the gathering, everyone will become friends or, at the very least, really good acquaintances. I once hosted a formal dinner with a couple of people that I learned didn't care for each other. I liked them both, so I risked bringing them together, and by the end of the night, they were exchanging numbers and making plans to get together.

For formal dinners, I opt to incorporate notes of gold in the decorative elements. Although silver is fine, my sense is that this particular metallic color adds a little more refinement than others. I also like to weave in more moody colors like charcoal, eggplant, or other jewel tones to add a bit of drama to the tabletop.

You can set up a self-serve drink area on an adjacent buffet or credenza where you or your guests can easily access wine or other beverages.

It's also kind to suggest attire for this type of dining experience. If you're elevating the atmosphere and expect guests to attend in cocktail attire, let them know. No one wants to be the odd one out showing up in sweats when an elegant ensemble may be required.

PARTY PLANNING

Guest Count
4 to 16

The Right Invite

I prefer the personal touch here. Invite the guests via phone or in person and tell them you'll follow up with a little note or email with all the details. Formal dinner guests should always have the details in writing. Be sure to include attire requirements and don't be afraid to request a step up from casual. Maybe ask them to wear collared shirts, cocktail attire, or make it really fun and call for Hollywood glam. Some people appreciate an excuse to get dressed up.

Sample Colorway
Charcoal gray and champagne gold

Sample Flower
Orchid

Musical Vibe

Sophisticated and moody: Ronald Isley and Burt Bacharach collaboration, Wynton Marsalis, Sade, Miles Davis's *Kind of Blue*, Billie Holiday, Louis Armstrong

Essential Décor Checklist
Bone china place settings—if you have them
Elegant charger plates or place mats
Elegant flatware
Dark glasses or cut crystal glasses
Place card holders
Non-obstructive flowers
Cloth dinner napkins
Napkin rings
Salt and pepper holders
Candleholders
Serving dishes
Serving utensils
Optional barware

PAN-FRIED HADDOCK

This dish is lovely accompanied by tiny roasted potatoes and a green salad. Simple, elegant, easy. Although I have an affinity for haddock, there are many other fish species, like trout, halibut, snapper, and sole that would work just as well with this recipe.

Pour the bread crumbs into a shallow bowl. Rinse the haddock fillets under cold water and lightly pat them dry with paper towels. Cut the fish into 3- to 4-inch pieces.

Warm the olive oil in a large skillet over medium-high heat. Dredge each fillet in the bread crumbs, pressing each side into the bread crumbs to help them to adhere to the fish.

Place each fillet in the skillet, sprinkle with Lawry's Seasoned Salt, and let them cook for about 10 minutes. Once the fillet is golden brown on the underside, flip it onto the other side, sprinkle with more Lawry's, and cook for another 10 minutes, until golden brown. Place the fish on a serving dish.

You can keep the fish in the oven on warm until dinnertime. Garnish with parsley just before serving.

Serves 6

2 cups panko bread crumbs
2 pounds haddock fillet
2 tablespoons olive oil
Lawry's Seasoned Salt
Chopped parsley, for garnish

SUNDAY BRUNCH

Be it Mother's Day, a baby shower, Easter, a wedding shower, or just because, there are many great reasons to gather together for a spring brunch.

I am one of those folks who can eat breakfast at any time of day, so for me, a meal that incorporates the best of breakfast, lunch, and sometimes dinner is like hitting the food jackpot.

To balance out the main savory items at a brunch, I love featuring adorable petits fours. They always remind me of my teen years in Louisiana, where our neighborhood bakery would display a colorful assortment of these petit treats en masse. The tiny cakes were available in every flavor and iced in every color imaginable. It was a feast for the eyes, and I think "petits fours" is just fun to say too. When they are offered at a gathering, these festive little treats add a personal touch because each guest gets to choose their favorite colors and flavors.

The best springtime color palette is all about pastels, so here I'm opting for a soft ivory and pink pairing, which is a beautiful complement to the pale greens of the season's new growth. Think about the tone you want for your gathering. A rule of thumb is that the more layers a place setting has, the more formal it becomes. Wooden charger plates help lay a foundation and have a lighter and less formal feel than those made of metal. Dinner plates may be placed directly on top or stacked elsewhere if the brunch is buffet-style.

In this setting, I topped the plates with decorative napkin rings because they create an interesting focal point for the place setting, and if they're fun, they can bring a little joy to each person sitting at the table. Pair them with simple white napkins that will balance the look of the tablescape.

I have an obsession with place card holders because they immediately make guests feel special. In this fast-paced world, people want to feel remembered and valued as individuals, and placing their names on the table is the easiest way to achieve that. For this brunch, I chose little pewter chair name card holders that have elegance but also a bit of whimsy.

Before and after any sit-down meal, guests often stand and gather somewhere else, so it's not a bad idea to create a separate area on a console table or counter that ties in to the occasion. Here, I've created a drink and dessert station to serve as a place where guests can grab a mug, glass, or bite of a pear or pecan tart. And to make sure you are able to enjoy your event and not be distracted by directing and answering a lot of questions, post a list of displayed offerings adjacent to the food options so your visitors can make decisions without approaching you for an explanation. This will give you more time to focus on enjoying your guests.

Refreshing iced tea is a safe way to go for a cool drink that will appeal to most, and I love mine with a hint of mint. When I was a young girl, my grandmother used to grow droves of spearmint around the edge of her porch, and she would use it to make the most refreshing iced tea. When my family moved from New York to Louisiana,

TARTS
on
Pear
Cookies:Cream
Pecan

my mother carefully gathered sprouts of the mint plants and meticulously replanted them in our new yard. And then my father proceeded to accidentally mow it all down to nothingness when he cut the lawn one day. Fortunately, these days, you can easily find fresh mint plants in nurseries and even large grocery stores.

Using tinted drinking glasses is a great way to bring a bit of color and character to your tabletop. When I'm designing, I like to tie in a color to at least one or two more places in the setting to create continuity in the space. If I introduce an accent color in a room, I'll repeat it once or twice to create visual harmony. When you use color for just one item, it can stick out as if it doesn't belong.

As a designer, I'm known for incorporating statement elements that are unique to the client and become a memorable focal point. I'll imagine what element the guest or homeowner will notice first when they enter the room and think about what their reaction might be when they see it. Sometimes, going "big" really is better, so when I'm designing semiformal to formal tabletops, I often incorporate statuesque flowers to steal the show. Because of their height, they immediately gain the attention of anyone who walks into the room, and they can be appreciated whether the guest is standing or sitting. My faves are snapdragons, like the ones for this party, calla lilies, and gladiolas. If there were a runway show for flowers, they would be there for sure. You just can't help but appreciate their unapologetic beauty.

TARTS
Pear
Cookies: Cream
Pecan

PARTY PLANNING

Guest Count
6 to 16

The Right Invite
Text, phone, or email them

Sample Colorway
Blush pink and creamy white

Sample Flower
Snapdragons

Musical Vibe
Cheery: Whitney Houston, Mariah Carey, Ariana Grande, Little Big Town

Essential Décor Checklist
Charger plates (preferably ones that don't read too luxe)
Multitiered trays for pastries or muffins
Framed sign to list the dishes being served
Table runner
Flatware
Dinner plates
Tinted glasses
Dinner napkins
Decorative napkin rings
Whimsical place card holders and cards
Salt and pepper holders or shakers
Tall candleholders
Statuesque flowers
Serving dishes

MINT ICED TEA

This recipe can be doubled or tripled depending on the number of guests you are serving. Feel free to use black or green tea. If you prefer your tea with a stronger mint flavor, feel free to double the amount of leaves.

Tear the mint leaves in half. Place the tea bags and mint leaves in a large saucepan, add 1 quart of the water, and bring to a boil over high heat. Lower the heat, stir in the sugar, and simmer for 15 minutes.

Remove from the heat and strain out the mint leaves and tea bags. Add 1 quart of cold water and let sit for 30 minutes to cool. Transfer the mixture to a large pitcher and refrigerate for 2 hours.

Serve over ice and garnish with fresh mint leaves.

Serves 6 to 8

1 handful fresh mint leaves (at least 10), plus more for garnish

2 black or 3 green tea bags

2 quarts cold water

½ cup sugar

DELIGHTFULLY CASUAL DINNER

When I was working in corporate America, one of my work friends invited a couple of us colleagues and a few other friends over for a casual dinner. It was held at her condo in the Woodley Park area of Washington, DC. I remember sitting at her crowded kitchen table having an out-of-body experience trying to identify the feeling I was having.

think it was joyous intimacy, the kind you can get only when you're sitting so close to people that the goal of comfort goes out the window and all that's left is accommodation for the gathering. I remember that the conversation flowed and the evening was relaxed and fun.

In springtime, casual dinners can be held indoors and sometimes outdoors. They are most successful when the attendees number eight people or fewer in attendance and the setting is more intimate. One of the best things about them is they can be planned at the last minute to celebrate a promotion at work, a birthday, a new condo, or whatever strikes you.

For this kind of event, place settings are best if they are not over-the-top and lean toward nature, like grass-woven place mats and casual napkin rings. The natural materials immediately speak to a more relaxed setting. Simplicity is also the best approach to take when considering what to serve. Sometimes when the dinner offerings become too intricate and overly complicated, you run the risk of the meal not appealing to most guests, plus as host you spend all your time cooking instead of socializing.

A number of years back, one of my team members hipped me to an idea that one of her friends shared of what to do with leftover Thanksgiving turkey—you make lasagna with it. Genius! I subsequently created my own recipe and now use it year-round with roasted chicken. What I love about it is if I don't have the energy to make the chicken myself, I simply buy a precooked rotisserie chicken, which is just as good at the grocery store. The reason I love this lasagna for casual dinners is it's always a crowd-pleaser, and you can prep it the day before, pop it in the refrigerator overnight, and bake it an hour before your gathering. Add a garden salad and French bread, and you're done.

For casual dinners, you can also place mismatched glasses on the table in different colors or heights, if you like. Why? Why not? It just says whimsy is more important than perfection at this table. By the way, if you really want to signal to guests that a dinner is casual, place a few large, recycled jars on the table and fill them with a laid-back flower of your choice, like a gerbera daisy. This gives the signal that this is a relaxed gathering. We're just here to eat, chill, and have fun.

I love the impact that a colorful table runner makes too. In casual settings, one that is made of natural fibers, like linen or cotton, and that maybe has a country-esque pattern or feel, is ideal.

Just in case you're still prepping dinner while your besties arrive, you can place recycled yogurt jars filled with pistachio nuts or trail mix on the counter that they can nosh on while they chat with you before the meal is served.

By the way, these settings are also great for a Galentine's dinner or let's-just-get-to-know-each-other-better (no pressure) meal.

TOP LEFT: Lasagna or another homey casserole is the focal point. **TOP RIGHT:** Be sure to invite just a few of your besties. **BOTTOM LEFT:** Place nuts and other snacks in recycled jars or glasses. **BOTTOM RIGHT:** These flowers offer bright pops of cheerful color.

PARTY PLANNING

Guest Count
2 to 8

The Right Invite
A text or direct message (DM) is fine in this instance

Sample Colorway
Orange and green

Sample Flower
Gerbera daisy

Musical Vibe
Laid-back: H.E.R., SZA, Adele, Billie Eilish

Essential Décor Checklist
Grass-woven place mats

Complementary casual napkin rings

Large recycled jars for vases

Off-white plates

Cotton dinner napkins

Casual flatware

Colored glasses, if available

Bright-colored flowers

Grass-woven breadbasket (optional)

Whimsical salt and pepper servers (optional)

Colorful, casual table runner

Serving utensils

ROASTED CHICKEN LASAGNA

This dish can be prepared up to two days ahead and refrigerated until ready to bake. I love Victoria's Tomato Basil pasta sauce, but if your grocery store doesn't sell it, just choose your favorite. For the pasta, try San Giorgio No. 81, which is delicious. Though whichever you use, make sure it's oven-ready, which doesn't require you to cook it before you layer it with all the ingredients. I used a simple but decorative baking dish that doubles as a serving dish.

Preheat the oven to 375°F. Coat a 9-by-13-inch baking dish with cooking spray.

Pull the chicken off the bone in large pieces and sprinkle lightly with Creole seasoning. Set aside.

Spread a layer of pasta sauce in the baking dish. Spread a layer of chicken over the sauce. Spread a layer of onions and spinach over the chicken and sprinkle a thin layer of mozzarella cheese on top. Drizzle with the sauce. Place three pieces of uncooked pasta across the top, making sure they don't overlap. Layer with chicken, then onions and spinach, cover with sauce, and then a layer of mozzarella cheese. Sprinkle with Italian seasoning. Place three more pieces of uncooked pasta across the top, making sure they don't overlap. Layer with chicken, then onions and spinach, cover with sauce, and then a layer of mozzarella cheese. Sprinkle with Italian seasoning. Place three more pieces of uncooked pasta across the top, making sure they don't overlap. Cover the pasta with sauce. Spread a layer of sharp Cheddar cheese and a layer of mozzarella cheese over the top. Sprinkle with Italian seasoning.

Grease a sheet of aluminum foil and cover the baking dish, greased side down. Bake for 40 minutes.

Increase the heat to 450°F. Remove the foil and bake for an additional 10 minutes or until the cheese becomes slightly brown on top.

Let cool for 5 minutes, then cut into serving portions.

Serves 6

1 rotisserie chicken

Tony Chachere's Original Creole Seasoning

2 (24-ounce) jars pasta sauce

¼ onion, sliced thinly

6 ounces fresh spinach

4 cups shredded mozzarella cheese

2 (1-pound) packages oven-ready lasagna

Italian seasoning

1 ounce shredded sharp Cheddar cheese

summer

Aaahhh, yes, it has finally arrived—the season of sundresses, shorts, and bare feet. Summertime is synonymous with casual living, spending time outdoors, and catching up with friends and family. Mother Nature makes it possible for us to open the hatches and venture out to beaches, mountains, lakes, and with the greatest frequency, our backyards.

To celebrate this most wonderful season, I've shared four suggestions for gatherings that go from summer elegance, like a sit down garden party luncheon, to casual outdoor fun, like my classic backyard barbecue. Any of these events can be tailored to the number of people you want to invite and how formal or informal an atmosphere you'd like to enjoy. Also included is a lazy summer breakfast that's easy to prepare ahead of time and lets your vacationing guests wake up when they like and have a morning meal waiting for them when they are ready.

The natural summer landscape creates a gorgeous kind of backdrop that mankind hasn't a shot at competing with. I say let's take advantage of nature's incomparable beauty and gather in the midst of it.

LUSH GARDEN LUNCHEON

There is very little formality in summer, but every once in a while, it's nice to have an excuse to wear a pretty sundress or a collared shirt. Enter the garden luncheon. If you or someone you know has a well-tended garden or backyard, that's where you should have it. As a matter of fact, even if you don't have a garden, you can create a similar ambience on an apartment or condo balcony by just adding a few pretty potted plants or flowers.

Many years back I was touring the British countryside with my mother and sister and we visited a classic English garden at Leeds Castle on a gloomy and rainy day. We stole away for a treat at the café and opted for the berry crumble, which turned out to be absolute heaven on earth. To this day it remains one of our favorite desserts ever. More recently, I was reading a book by the queen of summer stories herself, Elin Hilderbrand, and woven within the story was an incredible recipe for—you guessed it—berry crumble. I adapted it to make it my own and now I serve it to friends and family all the time. I've included the recipe here because summer produces the freshest and most flavorful berries, and it's absolutely delicious.

When I was a girl in Louisiana, my friend Terrie and I would head to the sugarcane fields for fun. Fully armed with knives resembling machetes, we would come back home with a couple of stalks of sugarcane and a bag of blackberries. (And yes, we laugh now at the fact that our parents let us roam the streets swinging huge weapons at the ages of ten and eleven. We blame it on country living.) Anyway, we used to toss the blackberries in a bowl with evaporated milk and a little sugar and were delighted with our creation. So, even if you're not up to making the crumble, ramekins filled with fresh berries and topped with whipped cream make an attractive and tasty alternative.

This small-scale type of social gathering works ideally with no more than sixteen or twenty guests. It's perfect for a powwow for besties, a group of friends, or a wedding shower.

Since the gathering is garden-inspired, I like to incorporate loose foliage on the table. Small sprigs of branches from hedges can be tied with cord or ribbon around flatware, and plates and bowls can be accented with heads of pom flowers.

This luncheon is a slightly more sophisticated summer affair, so go ahead and serve your food on decent plates and glassware. Melamine plates are always an option too, as long as they are colorful and decorative. The essential décor item in this setting is a vibrant tablecloth. Channel Lilly Pulitzer and lay out a cloth that is colorful, bright, and cheery. Crisp white plates on this background will make any meal appear fresh and yummy.

ABOVE: Details like these silver shoe place card holders and tinted glasses give the event an eclective vibe.

MIXED BERRY CRUMBLE

This recipe is always a crowd pleaser. I prefer incorporating three types of berries. However, if you only have two on hand, the recipe works just as well. And if your guests have nut allergies, you can forego the pecans.

Preheat the oven to 350°F.

For the berries: In a large bowl, gently mix the strawberries, blueberries, raspberries, granulated sugar, and flour until combined. Fill individual ramekins or an 8-by-11-inch ceramic baking dish with an even layer of the mixture.

To make the crumble: In a separate bowl, mix the flour, granulated sugar, brown sugar, cinnamon, salt, oats, melted butter, and pecans until combined. Lightly sprinkle the topping over the berries until they are completely covered.

Bake the crumble for 50 minutes, or until the topping is golden brown. Let cool for about 45 minutes on a wire rack. Serve warm (not piping hot), topped with ice cream or whipped cream (if desired).

Serves 6 to 8

FOR THE BERRIES

1 quart fresh strawberries, hulled and halved

1 pint fresh blueberries

1 pint fresh raspberries

½ cup granulated sugar

3 tablespoons all-purpose flour

FOR THE CRUMBLE

1 cup all-purpose flour

¼ cup granulated sugar

½ cup packed brown sugar

¾ teaspoon ground cinnamon

¼ teaspoon salt

1 cup quick-cooking oats (not instant)

½ cup (1 stick) melted butter

½ cup pecans

FOR SERVING

Ice cream (optional)

Whipped cream (optional)

Y'ALL COME! SEAFOOD FEAST

Honestly, the crab feast and the crawfish boil have got to be some of the messiest—and most fun— gatherings ever. During my tween and teen years, I lived in Lutcher, a small Louisiana town located in the River Parishes region right along the Mississippi River. Attending a crawfish boil there was an authentic bayou experience not to be missed. It was a feast for the eyes, ears, and taste buds.

Imagine picnic tables covered with newspaper or brown paper and piles of bright red boiled crawfish amid well-seasoned sausage, summer corn, and potatoes. In the background, there is a combination of festive zydeco, R&B, or pop music as well as musical voices calling out, "Hey, baby! How ya mamma doin'?" Later, there may be a little dancing on top of the tables. Whether or not I engaged in this particular activity will remain a secret. My point is that these gatherings were raucous events and I loved them.

Now that I live in Maryland, I relive those moments by throwing a crab feast, a very popular activity in the Chesapeake Bay region. The execution is a little more subdued, but the relaxed, down-and-dirty, joyful spirit is still a mainstay.

Essential décor items for a crab feast or crawfish boil include rolls of brown paper to cover the tables and lots of mini plates and bowls to hold lemon slices, melted butter for dipping, and wet wipes to clean up messy fingers. Small buckets or mugs holding wooden hammers and other useful tools make it easy for your guests to go to work.

Some hosts use oversized platters to place the food on the table, while others prefer to simply dump all the food directly on top of the brown paper for guests to easily grab whatever they like. Either is perfectly acceptable. This is a hands-on affair, so no need for plates (which are often considered pretentious). Stock the tables with large pitchers of cool water so everyone can tame the heat from the spicy seasonings, if they need to.

For this kind of gathering, you want to estimate high when buying the crab or crawfish to be sure there is enough to go around. You'll be surprised at how fast it goes!

By the way, for those not located in a region with easy access to crawfish or crabs, this setup and atmosphere works just as well for an old-fashioned fish fry. In this case, just spread the fried fish out on platters and serve with tiny containers of tartar sauce.

Most importantly, at a crab feast, crawfish boil, or fish fry, any hint of pretense is banned. Showing up in anything other than a halter top or T-shirt and shorts is the surest way to be identified as a newbie. But, if you are expecting some rookies, identify a few friendly guests in advance who can joyfully assist the neophytes in the process of breaking open the crabs or crawfish.

PARTY PLANNING

Guest Count
8 to 50

The Right Invite
If you're up for it, holler. Word of mouth works best. This is an event where you tell your friends to bring along anyone they like. The more really is the merrier.

Sample Colorway
White and red

Sample Flower
Sunflowers or wildflowers in jars

Musical Vibe
Fun and a little (or a lot) Southern: the Neville Brothers, Maze, Buckwheat Zydeco, CJ Chenier, Beyoncé

Essential Décor Checklist
Mini plates and bowls for lemon slices, melted butter, and wet wipes
Mugs or small buckets for shell-cracking tools
Jars or glasses for water or other beverages
Rolls of brown butcher paper and tape or stones for paperweights
Large water pitchers
Platters
Lanterns
Paper towels (lots)
Large metal tubs or coolers for soda, bottled beer, and wine coolers
Red-and-white-checked picnic tablecloth (optional)

ABOVE, TOP: A table set up by the water offers the perfect atmosphere for this shindig. **ABOVE, BOTTOM:** Have small mallets and other tools ready, so guests can dig in and start cracking open these succulent crab.

CHILE-RUBBED CORN ON THE COB

It's not summer without corn on the cob, and this version really spices things up. It is really easy to make, and the chile adds a little zest to this finger-friendly summer veggie.

Place the corn into an 8-quart pot or Dutch oven. Fill the pot with water, fully submerging the corn. Add the milk, sugar, and salt and bring to a boil over high heat. Simmer for 30 minutes.

Drain the corn and, while still warm, roll each piece of corn in the melted butter and then lightly roll it in the chile powder. Arrange the corn on a large platter or place them freestyle, directly on the table on top of the butcher paper.

Serves 12

12 half ears fresh or frozen corn on the cob, shucked

½ cup milk

1 tablespoon sugar

2 teaspoons salt

4 tablespoons (½ stick) melted butter

⅓ cup chile powder

LAZY SUMMER BREAKFAST

We are so grateful for opportunities to separate from work, and whether we are enjoying full-on vacations or long weekends, sleeping in is one of the best benefits. If you have a host of family members visiting your beach house or your rental at the Hamptons or Martha's Vineyard (or any beach location), take advantage of this by opting for a lazy summer breakfast or brunch where coming down in the morning is stress-free. Guests can show up to nosh at their leisure and not at an allocated time.

The key to this kind of easy-breezy breakfast is to create a setting where folks can easily grab whatever vittles they want. Variety is crucial so that everyone has something that appeals to them. You may want to include overnight oatmeal or muesli with toppings, boiled eggs, an assortment of pastries, and a large bowl of perfectly ripe mixed berries, the ultimate summer fruit. You can offer the same array of items each morning or include one item that changes daily, such as a quiche or a frittata that you (or one of your other family members) can make the night before and easily pop in the oven in the morning. And of course, there should be plenty of coffee and tea available.

One of the cutest offerings I've seen at one of these breakfasts are small jars of plain or vanilla yogurt topped with blueberries and granola or pecans. I now save up the small glass yogurt containers that I've used throughout the year and upcycle them as tiny serving dishes. They can also be used to hold jam or apple butter. Just stick a little label on them and you're all set. Speaking of upcycling, you can also repurpose those previously used iced tea bottles and refill them with a variety of juices.

For these laid-back settings, I'm a sucker for table décor featuring a country casual look in colors that say, "Yes, bare feet and pj's are welcome here."

BELOW: Have the table set in advance, and guests will have everything they need to enjoy their breakfast.

PARTY PLANNING

Guest Count

8 to 16

The Right Invite

Announce to all your guests when they arrive that breakfast will be set out from 8:00 to 10:30, for example. If you have a large swarm of people and you're afraid you'll forget to tell someone, you may want to write it out on a piece of paper and place the note in a picture frame on the counter, tape it to the refrigerator door, or leave a note at their bedside.

Sample Colorway

Country blue and off-white

Sample Flower

Ranunculus

Musical Vibe

Upbeat and cheery: Rihanna, Taylor Swift, Doja Cat, Paramore

Essential Décor Checklist

Cereal bowls

Casual flatware

White cloth or paper napkins with a trim or striping detail

Grass-woven or other casual place mats

Mugs for coffee and tea

Small plates

Mini recycled jars for yogurt and jam

Water pitcher

Recycled glass iced tea bottles for juice

Picture frame and paper for the menu and/or instructions

Pastry tray(s)

Large bowl for mixed fruit

Varying height serving dishes and bowls

Small bowls for oatmeal or yogurt toppings

Linen table runner

SALMON AND SPINACH QUICHE

Cold cereal is fine, but there's nothing like having the option of a warm dish for breakfast. Feel free to substitute ham or bacon for meat lovers. In this case, removing the spinach is optional. Almost every time I serve this, people take more than one slice, so that's why this makes two quiches.

Preheat the oven to 375°F.

Remove any bones and skin from the salmon and flake off pieces with a fork. Spread the salmon over the bottom of the pie shells.

In a separate bowl, beat the eggs. Add the milk, onion, cheese, salt, and pepper and stir until combined. Mix in the shredded spinach. Divide the mixture between the two pie shells and bake for 50 minutes or until firm.

The quiche can be served at room temperature or kept warm on a warming tray.

Serves 6 to 8

8 ounces cooked salmon

2 frozen 9-inch pie shells

8 eggs

1½ cups milk

½ onion, minced

1 cup shredded Cheddar or Colby Jack cheese

1 teaspoon seasoned salt

Pinch of pepper

3 handfuls fresh spinach, shredded

Breakfast
8AM - 10AM

Serve
Yourself

BACKYARD BARBECUE

When I was a little girl, my grandfather would throw these huge family barbecues every summer on Long Island, New York. It was always great to see family members of all ages we hadn't seen in a while. As a child, I had such a sense of independence because we were unmonitored and allowed to run around freely, and even better, we could stay outside after dark to play games and chase fireflies. As I think about it now, that may have been my first taste of what freedom felt like.

There was also something so dreamy about the smell of meat and vegetables cooking over charcoal or mesquite. These intoxicating aromas let us know there were some good eats on the way. And amidst the upbeat music that was always played loudly, there was also the constant sound of hearty, unrestrained laughter. I can't remember attending one cookout where I wasn't greeted with an exuberant smile or hello. This was the pinnacle of relaxed summer togetherness.

To create your own cookout, prepping the day before is critical, because the goal is to spend your time enjoying the festivities, not running around the whole time cooking and organizing.

Unless you're expecting just a few guests, decorative paper plates are fine as long as they are sturdy. No one wants barbecue sauce seeping through to their summer whites. Setting out a buffet-style table, preferably in a shady spot, will work well. Small placards on stands can be used to identify condiments and each dish being served. Keeping cold food chilled is essential, and I really like the servers that are on the market now that allow you to place ice in a bottom section to keep the temperature cool. Iced tea, lemonade, and water dispensers are great go-tos because most are also easy for kids to operate on their own. They can also be easily marked by hanging tags to distinguish each drink. Keep a bowl of wet wipes around so guests can clean sticky hands easily.

One dish that I serve regularly and my friends rave about is my rack of barbecued ribs. But the thing is—they're really not mine. Years back, I saw master music producer Quincy Jones being interviewed by Oprah Winfrey, and he shared with the audience his incredible recipe for ribs that were marinated and cooked to perfection. I put my own spin on them, and they never fail to be a crowd-pleaser.

BELOW, LEFT: Use paper plates and napkins in vibrant hues. **BELOW, RIGHT:** Bright-tinted glasses complement the blues of the striped tablecloth.

TOP: Use screened covers to keep flies and other pests away from the food.
BOTTOM, LEFT: Reusable small signs identify condiments. **BOTTOM, RIGHT:** This casual setting cries out for daisies.

PARTY PLANNING

Guest Count
6 to 30

The Right Invite
This is a laid-back event, so text or call your guests. Avoid formal invitations that won't communicate the relaxed nature of the gathering.

Sample Colorway
Lime green and lemon yellow

Sample Flower
Daisies

Musical Vibe
Bob Marley, Jimmy Cliff, Beyoncé, Drake, Bad Bunny.
If this is a large affair, level up with a live steel drum band.

Essential Décor Checklist
White daisies for the tables and place settings
Bamboo or plastic utensils
Bamboo decorative paper plates, or melamine plates
Coordinating paper napkins
Large drink dispensers
Chilled food servers
Drink placards and holders
Condiment containers
Small condiment placards
Large serving platters
Cotton or vinyl tablecloth(s)
Protective food tents
Tongs and other serving utensils

LORNA'S SMACKIN' GOOD RIBS

One of the great things about these ribs is they can be prepared up to two days in advance and left to chill in the fridge before cooking, which helps if you'll be busy doing many other things in the days preceding your cookout. These ribs are really tender. Take care to cut them carefully so that each section stays in tact.

Line two large roasting pans with enough foil to tightly wrap the ribs. Spray the foil with cooking spray. Spread a layer of the peppers and onions directly on the foil.

Rinse the racks of ribs and pat them dry with a paper towel. Pat 1 tablespoon of garlic on the underside of the first rack of ribs and sprinkle heavily with Creole seasoning. Lay the seasoned side directly on the vegetables. Pat 1 tablespoon of garlic on the top side of the ribs and sprinkle heavily with the seasoning. Spread a layer of the peppers and onions on top. Repeat the process with the other rack of ribs. Tightly wrap the ribs in the foil and refrigerate for at least 16 hours.

On the morning of the barbecue, preheat the oven to 400°F. Remove the pans from the refrigerator and let the ribs sit at room temperature for 30 minutes.

Lower the oven temperature to 300°F. Place the pans of ribs in the oven and bake for 6 to 8 hours, until the meat is almost falling off the bone.

Preheat a gas or charcoal grill.

Remove the ribs from the oven and gently uncover them. Baste the top of the ribs with barbecue sauce. Cover with the foil again and transfer the ribs to the grill. Poke holes in the top of the foil and cook on the grill rack for 15 minutes.

Remove and cut the ribs between each bone with a sharp knife. Serve on a large platter with tongs.

Serves 10 to 12

Cooking spray

1 green bell pepper, seeded and thinly sliced

1 red bell pepper, seeded and thinly sliced

1 yellow bell pepper, seeded and thinly sliced

1 large yellow or Vidalia onion, halved and thinly sliced

2 racks of ribs (3 to 4 pounds each), preferably St. Louis style

4 tablespoons chopped or minced garlic

Tony Chachere's Original Creole Seasoning

Sweet Baby Ray Barbecue Sauce

~ fall ~

The season for harvesting is upon us. Autumn offers us a few final opportunities to capitalize on temperate weather. It's a season to calm down from a highly active sunny-day pace and to store and gather up everything we need for the inclement weather ahead. Did someone say "gather"? From Thanksgiving to Diwali to Rosh Hashanah to "just because we want to," there are so many reasons to come together during this incredible season.

The crisp autumn air and atmosphere seem like a wake-up call. This season is the time to determine what to harvest and what to let go of. I find myself lamenting the warm weather soon to be gone and simultaneously looking forward to cuddling up with a cup of tea or a mug of hot cider.

Either way, this season gives us a chance to take one last stab at hanging together outdoors and then leads us to (gratefully) come back inside.

~ fall ~

COZY AFTERNOON TEA

Early autumn is an ideal time to catch up with one or a few friends and swap stories about everything you did over the summer. No need for a big meal here. The afternoon tea is great for reconnecting with your besties whom you may have missed while you were enjoying vacations filled with activities and travels.

There is something that is so calming about tea. It's been a mainstay in my family for as long as I can remember, and it's often used as a cure for stomachaches, headaches, and even heartaches—especially if it's served up in a cute cup.

Evidently, we can thank the Duchess of Bedford, Anna Maria Russell, who in the 1840s felt as if there was too much time between lunch and a late dinner. So, she began a mini afternoon meal, which we know fondly as afternoon tea.

Once when I was visiting London, my colleague took me to high tea at the Savoy Hotel. That was a memorable event, complete with scones and clotted cream, cucumber sandwiches, and tiny delectable pastries. The experience was a joy and I became an even worse tea addict from that moment on. While on a business trip to Japan, I was wooed by roasted-rice tea, and when visiting a client in Oman, I enjoyed sumptuous tea with cardamon. Today, I seek out English, Asian, and global-influenced tea hotels, shops, and cafes wherever I live or travel.

Afternoon tea with friends is a level up from just lunch. It is an *experience*. For that reason, if you are a tea lover, you should absolutely have a tea set that includes a teapot, at least four teacups and saucers, a sugar dish, and a creamer. You don't have to spend a mint on it. Cute tea sets can be found at specialty shops, online, or at thrift and consignment stores. If you're into it, you can also procure an antique set.

Create your own afternoon tea by pulling together a few light sandwiches and cutting them into thirds or quarters. No crust, please. Order a variety of scones and bite-size pastries from your nearest bakery. Or you can choose to make your own baked goods. My daughter's good friend, who is also a tea enthusiast, makes the most delightful lavender tea cookies. They are so light and leave you with a fragrant aftertaste.

Whether you decide to make or purchase your goodies, keep in mind that presentation is everything, and the three-tiered serving curate stand is the grande dame. The display immediately makes whatever you're serving appear special. Tradition is to place sandwiches and other savories on the bottom, scones in the middle, and pastries on the top tier. A standard afternoon tea can be served at a low coffee or cocktail table. High tea, which tends to have more hearty offerings, is usually served at a "higher" dining table. Either works fine.

OPPOSITE, TOP: A beautiful tea set is the focal point of this gathering. OPPOSITE, BOTTOM: A tart perched on a tall stand gives the table interest and dimension.

PARTY PLANNING

Guest Count
2 to 6

The Right Invite
Give your close friends a ring. They'll be thrilled to come see you.

Sample Colorway
Soft whites

Sample Flower
Mixed bouquet

Musical Vibe
Classic: Natalie Cole, Frank Sinatra, Ella Fitzgerald, Terence Blanchard

Essential Décor Checklist
Flowers
Fresh greenery
Small glasses or vases to use for single blooms
Cake stand (optional)
Three-tiered curate stand
Teacups and saucers
Decorative sandwich plates
Teapot
Teaspoons
Sugar bowl and creamer
Cloth napkins
Small tablecloth
Decorative ribbon (optional) to decorate the curate stand

LAVENDER TEA COOKIES

Everybody loves a melt-in-your-mouth shortbread cookie. I've elevated these to party status by adding a little lavender. For a lovely presentation, I like to dust the tops of the cookies with additional crushed lavender after I place them on the serving dish. In design, we always say the difference is in the details. And so it is with food, as well.

In a stand mixer or using an electric mixer, cream the butter until fluffy, about 4 minutes.

Add the granulated sugar, powdered sugar, salt, vanilla, and 2 teaspoons of the crushed lavender and mix until well combined.

With the mixer on low, slowly add the flour and mix just until combined. It's okay if the dough seems dry. Transfer the mixture to a work surface and, using your hands, form it into a log about 1½ inches in diameter. Wrap the log in plastic wrap and chill in the refrigerator for 2 hours.

Preheat the oven to 350°F. Line a baking sheet with parchment paper.

Cut the log into ½-inch slices and place them on the prepared baking sheet, making sure they don't touch. They won't spread much. Top each cookie with a sprinkle of the remaining crushed lavender and some coarse sugar.

Bake for 15 minutes. Turn the baking sheet 180 degrees and continue to bake for another 10 minutes, or until the cookies are browned on the bottom.

Let cool slightly on the baking sheet, then transfer to a wire rack and let cool completely. To serve, place the cookies on a serving dish and dust the top with a little more of the crushed lavender.

Makes 20 to 25 cookies

1 cup (2 sticks) butter

¼ cup granulated sugar

¼ cup powdered sugar

1 teaspoon salt

1 teaspoon vanilla extract

4 teaspoons crushed food-grade lavender , plus more as desired

2 cups all-purpose flour

Coarse decorative sugar

~ fall ~

FRIENDSGIVING OUTDOOR DINNER

September through mid-October is a great time to host the last outdoor gathering of the year. Most of the bugs have, thankfully, begun to head out of town for the season and the stickiness of summer is long gone.

One of my clients hosts an annual harvest dinner in the middle of October in the courtyard of their home in Georgetown, DC. The setup is easy and elegant as well as festive.

L arge lanterns adorn the table, and the glow from the candlelight highlights the food and kisses the faces of all the guests with its warm glow. I look forward to the intimate event and see it as a thankful sign-off to warm days for a while.

One of the genius executions of this event is that the host takes care of the main course and dessert, while each guest brings a side dish. There is always a beautiful cornucopia of food selections, and often the guests discuss the origins of their dishes—one may be a beloved recipe from a great-grandmother while another is a tasty discovery from a local market. It's all good.

If you live in a more northern climate, it is great to begin these dinners right at sunset so the guests can enjoy the gathering a bit before it gets too nippy outside. You can also drape shawls on every other chair or over a post just in case someone needs to wrap up a bit.

A crisp white or linen tablecloth is a décor essential if your goal is to create a more elegant or sophisticated evening. Glasses in a color of the season are a good approach or crystal wineglasses pair well with candlelight as they reflect the amber light beautifully. Classic white or off-white plates on chargers are a timeless choice for a lovely place setting. No need to incorporate obvious color.

Color and interest can be added to the table by placing artistically designed salad plates on top of simple white or off-white dinner plates. Eucalyptus leaves can add more color and accent each table setting by tucking them around each plate or into napkin rings. Autumn flowers like mums tend to be plentiful this time of year, so feel free to adorn the table with them to achieve pops of brilliant color.

If your outdoor dinner goes on past sunset, definitely opt for large candle lanterns that add so much ambience and warmth. Name cards on woven place card holders add a nice touch and make each guest feel like they've been thoughtfully considered. Finally, if you happen to have a large-scale wooden or woven sculptural piece that you can place on the table, go for it. This kind of accent can add an unexpected touch or sense of whimsy.

PARTY PLANNING

Guest Count
8 to 24

The Right Invite
Email invitations

Sample Colorway
Amber

Sample Flower
Mums

Musical Vibe
Brazilian, neo-soul, or sophisticated music:
Bossa Nova for Lovers EP, Maxwell, Snoh Aalegra, Boney James

Essential Décor Checklist
Off-white or natural wooden chargers or place mats
Place cards and holders
Candleholders and lanterns in varying heights
Colored wineglasses
Classic white or off-white dinner plates
Artistic salad plates
Flatware
White, off-white, or natural fiber tablecloth
Cloth dinner napkins
Decorative napkin rings
Salt and pepper holders
Brightly colored mums or other flowers and complementary foliage
Tall, narrow vases for flowers
Large decorative object for centerpiece
Shawls or throws for guests to stay warm (optional)

ABOVE, CLOCKWISE FROM TOP LEFT: Wicker place card holders and the table linens offer a variety of textures. The wooden rocking horse makes a whimsical statement. Botanical plates give a basic table character.

AU GRATIN POTATOES

This is a warm and filling side dish that is a real crowd-pleaser, plus it goes well with most other main dishes or vegetable sides, making it good for a party like this where everyone contributes.

Place the potatoes in a large pot or Dutch oven, add salted water to cover, and bring to a boil over medium-high heat. Cook until tender when pierced with a knife, about 1 hour. Drain and let cool for 1 hour. (The potatoes can be cooked a day ahead and refrigerated overnight, if preferred.)

Preheat the oven to 375°F. Coat a medium to large casserole dish with cooking spray.

Peel the potatoes and cut them into ¼-inch slices. Spread a layer of potatoes in the prepared baking dish. Spread a layer of onions over the potatoes. Place four or five pats of butter on top. Sprinkle some flour, salt, and pepper over the onion. Repeat the process for two more layers. Pour the milk over the top and sprinkle with the Cheddar cheese. Cover the dish with the top of the casserole dish or aluminum foil and bake for 45 minutes. Take off the foil and bake for another 5 to 10 minutes, or until the cheese is browned.

Serve with the bacon bits in a small bowl alongside the potatoes.

Serves 12 to 16

2 pounds Russet potatoes

Salt

Cooking spray

⅓ onion, thinly sliced

½ cup (1 stick) salted butter

⅓ cup all-purpose flour

Pepper

1½ cups milk

¾ cup grated sharp Cheddar cheese

Bacon bit crumbles, for garnish (optional)

A BLESSED THANKSGIVING FEAST

Once a year we gather together to express our gratitude for the bounty that we have received, and Thanksgiving is that moment.

The most critical aspect of this occasion is making every attendee feel like they are valued and important. I remember being relegated to the children's table when I was a kid, but I broke that tradition when I became an adult and began hosting Thanksgiving in my own home.

think it's a growth opportunity for children to be exposed to discussions of current events and interesting topics—even if it's through osmosis. After all, very little conversation would happen at the kids' table these days, anyway. They would be sitting there with a fork in one hand and their phone in the other. No eye contact. Just an occasional chuckle in response to the latest social media post.

To make guests feel important, be sure that everyone has a place card—even the youngsters. They'll get a kick out of seeing that someone featured their name too. And speaking of name cards, try to be strategic about placement if you know there is tension between family members. My philosophy is don't sit them too far apart or right next to each other, but seat them close enough that there is a chance to mend fences over a great meal. It doesn't hurt to also have a couple of amusing "remember the time" stories ready to get the chatter going.

My thinking regarding styling the table is that we don't need to be relegated to the same old traditional Thanksgiving colorways. It is perfectly fine to mix it up a bit by bringing in other rich colors, like aubergine and touches of gold.

Snip the stems off some flowers and place just the blooms at the corners of each plate to soften the hard surfaces of the dinnerware. At this time of year it's easy to find cloth napkins that have a special message or intricate detail, and you can tuck the top of the napkin between plates and hang the bottom portion slightly over the table. Let the whole table gleam by setting out your finest serving utensils and tall, thin candleholders to add a little sparkle.

This is the type of big occasion where you can enlist support from the other attendees by having them bring side dishes and desserts, which will keep you from getting completely worn out from all the preparation and cooking. People love to share their treasured favorites at Thanksgiving. Be sure to have extra serving ware and utensils on hand for the food that others bring.

Tradition ranks highly for this holiday, so feature your best bone china, and if it's a set that goes back generations in your family, even better. The turkey (of course) is the star of the show. Delicious side dishes act as essential supporting cast members and it wouldn't be Thanksgiving without them. My favorite Thanksgiving tables are those that are fully loaded with every dish with the turkey in the center, so that food must be passed. When people pass dishes around the table, one person must always help another, sometimes in very subtle ways, and it's a gesture of caring and community. That is what Thanksgiving is—a gathering of people who care about each other and want to celebrate their blessings together.

Gratefulness abounds. Blessed food, blessed world, blessed life.

PARTY PLANNING

Guest Count
6 to 16

The Right Invite
Call and text invitations

Sample Colorway
Aubergine and gold

Sample Flower
Chrysanthemums and snapdragons

Musical Vibe
Cross-generational/transcendent: Earth, Wind & Fire,
instrumental, Adele, Elton John, Stevie Wonder

Essential Décor Checklist
Your best legacy china
Crystal glassware
Place cards and holders
Metallic charger plates
Tall, thin candles and holders
Cloth napkins with optional messaging
Your best flatware
Serving utensils plus extras
Serving dishes
Tablecloth
Autumnal table runner
Tall flowers plus poms for the plates
Tall vases

SWEET POTATO PIE

This pie is a Southern classic that is tasty served warm or cool and everyone loves it—young and old. The recipe makes two pies, so it's good for a crowd. Serve as is or with whipped cream or scoops of ice cream if you like.

Preheat the oven to 375°F.

Whisk the eggs in a large bowl. Add the sweet potatoes, butter, sugar, flour, evaporated milk, lemon extract, and vanilla and mix until well combined. Divide the mixture between the pie shells. Place each pie on individual baking sheets. Bake for 45 minutes, or until the center appears firm. Let cool for 15 minutes. Cut into slices and serve warm or at room temperature.

Serves 12 to 16

3 eggs

2½ cups mashed sweet potatoes (4 or 5 potatoes)

½ cup (1 stick) butter, melted

¾ cup sugar

3 tablespoons all-purpose flour

1 cup evaporated milk

1 teaspoon lemon extract

1 teaspoon vanilla extract

2 frozen 9-inch pie shells

Mango C S

Veggie R

LaLam

Rum

CHIC COCKTAIL PARTY

The few weeks preceding the official start of winter mark the height of cocktail party season. Back when I worked in corporate America, our advertising agency would invite its clientele to an annual formal event at the Drake Hotel in Chicago. It was a treat to see our colleagues in their Friday night best among gorgeously set tables with chic décor. Now that so many aspects of our lives have become more casual, it's a rare pleasure to have an excuse to dress up in clothing that makes you look and feel special.

You can consider giving your cocktail party a light theme, like suggesting that everyone come wearing something winter white, classic black, or a mask. I also love when a signature drink is featured. One cocktail party my firm hosted allowed guests to tour a home that we designed with an art deco interior. The Southern term for this kind of party is a "Sip and See" and we offered food within that theme that would have been served during the 1930s along with a popular drink from that era called a Soixante Quinze (nowadays called a French 75). We also featured music from the era with a live musician.

If you decide to host a cocktail party in your home, clear out multiple areas where groups of four or five people can gather together to talk comfortably. Placing hors d'oeuvres and drinks at standing height can make it much more convenient for your guests. Finger food is critical, meaning that it can be consumed in one bite while standing, without requiring utensils. After all, who wants to juggle a drink, a plate, and a utensil when you have only two hands? Opt for tall, statuesque flowers, like gladiolas, that make a statement and can be appreciated while standing.

This is one of those gatherings where enlisting a little help can make all the difference. Passed food is always a nice and convenient touch, so consider hiring a catering company or even a couple of college students (over the age of twenty-one) to help out.

BELOW, LEFT: A cheese plate is always welcome at a cocktail party. BELOW, RIGHT: Offer bite-size appetizers that don't require utensils.

Ensure that there are a variety of drinks so there is something for everyone—wine, cocktails, and nonalcoholic beverages like sparkling water, still water, high-end juices, or mocktails should be readily accessible. A bartender can help manage the flow of cocktails and mocktails. A live jazz musician or ensemble can help create a higher level of elegance and a more memorable experience. Guests will feel like it was worth taking all the extra time to look as fantastic as they do.

This is the type of gathering where it's actually better to invite a lot of people to keep the atmosphere buzzing with conversation. If it's in your budget, definitely hire a bartender who is knowledgeable and savvy at mixing drinks and understands how to prepare your featured drinks. Depending on the party theme, cocktail napkins with witty sayings or images can add some extra cheer to the gathering.

You can easily make guests aware of what their food and drink options are by writing out small menus and placing them in picture frames that stand on the tables.

A lovely cheese board or charcuterie board is appealing to most anyone and makes a nice statement. Have at least three cheese offerings to start: one hard, like Manchego or Gouda; one soft, like Brie; and one wild card, like an herbed goat cheese or Havarti. You may add slices of hard salami or prosciutto. Small bunches of grapes and little bowls of Marcona almonds or spiced pecans are also nice additions.

PARTY PLANNING

Guest Count
20 to 50

The Right Invite
Because people's schedules are so full this time of year,
I strongly recommend sending save-the-date notices
ahead of time. Then email or mail festive invitations.

Sample Colorway
White with subtle black and metallic accents

Sample Flower
Gladiolas

Musical Vibe
Live musician such as an acoustic guitarist or saxophonist or
related to the party theme or a mix of jazz and retro classics

Essential Décor Checklist
Drink decanter
Carafe(s) for assorted beverages
Festive cocktail napkins
Various wine, champagne, and drink glasses
Wineglass stem rings (optional)
Large vases for tall flowers
Tall flowers, like gladiolas or orchids
Ice bucket(s)
Tongs
Multitiered serving dishes
Cheese board with serving utensils
Candleholders and candles of various heights
Small picture frames for menus

SOIXANTE QUINZE

This drink is more widely known today as a French 75, and it is a classic cocktail served in the South. It's fresh and lemony, and any drink made with Champagne is extra festive. Make it in a batch ahead of time so you can have it ready to go when your guests arrive.

In a small saucepan over medium heat, combine the sugar and water. Cook, stirring often, until the sugar is completely dissolved. Set the simple syrup aside to cool completely.

In a large pitcher, mix together the gin, lemon juice, and cooled simple syrup and mix well. Refrigerate until ready to serve.

Add the Champagne, ice cubes, and lemon slices and serve immediately.

Serves 8

¾ cup sugar

¾ cup water

2 cups gin

1 cup lemon juice

4 cups chilled Champagne or sparkling dry white wine

Ice cubes

Lemon slices

RUM BALLS

A classic for the winter holidays, rum balls are small round treats that are perfect for a cocktail party because you can eat them in one bite. I've been making this recipe for family and friends since I was a teenager. This recipe is incredibly simple, they can be made in advance, they taste so good, and no cooking is required!

In a bowl, combine the vanilla wafers, cocoa, syrup, rum, and pecans and mix well. Shape the mixture into 1-inch balls (bite-size) and place them on a platter. Refrigerate for 24 hours. Just before serving, roll each rum ball in powdered sugar. Arrange on a plate and serve.

Serves 16 to 24

1 pound vanilla wafers, crushed

1 tablespoon unsweetened cocoa powder

½ cup Karo syrup

¼ cup brown rum

½ cup chopped pecans

Powdered sugar

ABOVE, CLOCKWISE FROM TOP: Set up a separate beverages table. Cheeky cocktail napkins keep the party light.

winter

You know those annoying people who start playing holiday music in October? Well, I'm one of them. I am so drawn to the cheer of this holiday that I just can't help myself from letting everyone know that the season of joy is finally upon us. There's something so uplifting about its focus on hope, giving, and fellowship.

There's also something alluring about having an excuse like cold weather to retreat from the hustle and bustle of life and slow down the pace for a while. There aren't many moments in life that are more peaceful than cuddling next to a warm fire and getting cozy with a great book or great person or gathering at home with your favorite people. And let's not forget that 'tis the season for comfort food that soothes the soul with every bite.

FROSTY HOLIDAY DINNER

Whether you are religious or not, the holiday season is a beautiful time to gather together and celebrate human connection and the ending of a great year. (And if the year wasn't so great, that's even more reason to be happy that it's over!)

Maybe it's the lights or the music or the decorations, but there is something about the sparkle and joy of the season that is mesmerizing. All the more reason to have some friends over while beauty abounds and when joy is in the air.

I love holiday parties and dinners that occur early or very late in December, either before the holiday or after the hustle and bustle of the season when we are no longer stressed and juggling absolutely everything.

That being said, Christmas Eve is another opportunity to host a special event while avoiding any family gathering conflicts on Christmas Day itself. If you decide to host Christmas Eve dinner, you can opt for a somewhat casual setting, unless this night marks the formal dinner for your family (which is the case in many Latino and Italian traditions). Hearty soups or make-ahead casseroles warm the soul and make hosting that much easier.

Although I don't celebrate Hanukkah, I have friends who do, and as a little girl I secretly envied the idea of receiving a gift eight days in a row. Obviously, the holiday means more than that, and as an adult I love the true meaning of Hanukkah, which was built around an historical event where a one-day supply of oil to light a temple candle actually lasted for eight days. There is an emphasis on hopefulness and optimism that makes the perfect atmosphere for celebration.

Kwanzaa is another holiday that utilizes the lighting of candles to reinforce various principles. Most often celebrated by African Americans, this holiday emphasizes culture, community, family, and history. All these holidays, the season itself, and the lighting of candles help us to remember to love, to hope, and to consider how even the darkest moments can glow if a little light shines on them.

I recommend decorating the table with candles, winter-inspired centerpieces, and other décor pieces shortly after Thanksgiving, so you can check off that box early. Using colorways based in whites and silver is an elegant way to go. The palette is suitable for guests from any background or religion and can be accented with virtually any other color, if you like.

Place settings can be a crisp white with a little frosty silver. Decorate your table with a host of tealights or votive candles, placed amidst green foliage for a little softening and contrast. If you're feeling ambitious, you can pick up some twigs from the woods and spray-paint them silver. As a final, but super-easy, touch, grab a few sprigs of evergreen to adorn the place settings.

PARTY PLANNING

Guest Count
6 to 10

The Right Invite
Email, text, or printed—depending on how formal you would like to be

Sample Colorway
White and silver

Sample Flower
Ruscus and Leyland greenery

Musical Vibe
Vince Guaraldi, Tchaikovsky, or holiday music with cultural significance

Essential Décor Checklist
White or white and silver tablecloth
Tealights or votive candles
Winter centerpiece décor, such as a small tree or ceramic reindeer
Fresh green winter foliage
Dinnerware
Silver or white charger plates
Flatware
Wine and drinking glasses
White patterned cloth napkins
Napkin rings or metallic cord

ABOVE, TOP LEFT: Shimmery silver details support the festive tablescape.
ABOVE, TOP RIGHT: White on white on white creates a winter wonderland.
ABOVE, BOTTOM: Sprigs of evergreen offer beautiful color and aroma.

BUTTERNUT SQUASH SOUP

This soup is yummy and soothing to the soul. It smells so good and it'll warm you up when there's a chill in the air.

Melt the butter in a large pot over medium heat, add the onion, and sauté until tender, about 10 minutes. Add the squash, pears, broth, and thyme and bring to a boil, stirring often. Lower the heat to a simmer and continue to cook until the squash and pears are tender, about 15 minutes.

Carefully transfer the mixture to a blender or food processer and purée until smooth. Pour the mixture back into the pot and stir in the vanilla, whipping cream, salt, and pepper. Cook, stirring occasionally, until heated through.

Serve the soup in individual bowls and sprinkle each serving with pumpkin seeds and a dash of nutmeg.

Serves 6

2 tablespoons butter

¾ cup chopped onion

1 pound butternut squash, peeled and cut into 1-inch cubes

3 pears, peeled, cored, and sliced

2 cups chicken broth

2 teaspoons fresh thyme

1 teaspoon vanilla extract

1 cup whipping cream

¼ teaspoon salt

¼ teaspoon pepper

⅓ cup pumpkin seeds

½ teaspoon ground nutmeg

FORMAL CHRISTMAS DINNER

In the River Parishes area of Louisiana where I grew up, the lead-up to Christmas is a big thing. For weeks the locals build enormous artistic bonfires on the levees that line the Mississippi River. When the sun sets on Christmas Eve, they burn the bonfires to light Santa Claus's way to the homes in the area. Residents from the community and visitors from miles around travel to see the sights and gather to join in a host of festivities.

My family also celebrates Christmas Eve by attending a candlelight church service and singing Christmas carols—a great reminder of "the reason for the season." By the time Christmas Day arrives, we are all in.

Almost every year, I host a large formal dinner for family and friends on Christmas night. This is not a T-shirt-and-jeans affair. I try to make this a real occasion, and my goal is that everyone who attends feels special. The holidays are full of ritual, pomp, and circumstance, so I figure, why not go with it?

I set the table one or two days ahead of time, which allows me to give a lot of thought to where everyone will be seated. Each year, I try to mix it up a bit by seating guests next to someone they know really well and someone they may not know as well. I also like to invite someone who may otherwise be alone for the holiday. Even if they decline the invitation, they know that they are thought of highly. To that end, each place has a name card, which conveys that each person is valued and special.

One way to bring the beauty of the Christmas tree to the table is to hang ornaments from a chandelier that hangs above or by filling an oversized decorative basket or bowl with spectacular ornaments. If they are fragile, carefully lay them on a nest of foliage. Gift-wrap small empty boxes and run them down the center of the table or place small wrapped gifts in front of each place setting.

Place glitzy ornaments around the plates or napkins to add another touch of glam to the occasion. At a Christmas dinner like this, the food is bountiful, the music is flowing, the candles are lit, and the conversation abounds.

PARTY PLANNING

Guest Count
8 to 18

The Right Invite
Call or text

Sample Colorway
Green or teal, berry red, and gold

Sample Flower
Holly berries, greenery, poinsettias

Musical Vibe
Holiday music: Vanessa Williams, Nat King Cole, Boyz II Men, Kelly Clarkson

Essential Décor Checklist
Elegant white charger plates
Your best china
Colorful/artistic accent plates
Formal flatware
Elegant gold place mats
White textured cloth napkins
Crystal glassware
Ornaments with strings or ribbons
Large bowl for collection of ornaments
Fresh greenery for bowl
Candleholders and candles
Small gift-wrapped boxes in silver or teal (optional)

ABOVE, TOP: Simple ornaments pack a colorful punch as a centerpiece.
ABOVE, BOTTOM: Layering plates and a charger add to the formality of this event, while the colorful salad plate tempers that with some quirkiness.

CRANBERRY RELISH

Here is a twist on a classic found on almost all holiday tables. I love it even more for its gorgeous color, which complements the colorway of this party.

In a medium bowl, dissolve the Jell-O in the boiling water. While the mixture is still warm, add the cranberry sauce and mix until melted.

Measure ½ cup of the reserved pineapple juice. If there isn't enough, add enough cold water to reach ½ cup. Add the pineapple juice mixture, crushed pineapple, lemon juice, and nuts and stir until well combined.

Pour the mixture into a decorative ceramic or clear glass bowl and chill until set, about 5 hours.

Serve directly from the bowl.

1 (6-ounce) package strawberry Jell-O

1 cup boiling water

1 (16-ounce) can whole cranberry sauce

1 (16-ounce) can crushed pineapple, juices reserved

2 teaspoons lemon juice

½ cup chopped pecans

POST-CHRISTMAS BREAKFAST

The day after Christmas, there's usually a bunch of folks still at my house, which is fine with me—especially because the crowd is often made up of children. I see the morning after as the last hurrah of family togetherness. Everyone is relaxed and refreshed from all the excitement from the previous day.

To make the breakfast table appear more relaxed, grab a handful of ornaments off the tree and scatter them around the table. You can also place a swirl of some ribbon (possibly saved from unwrapped gifts from the day before) on the table for a little whimsy.

Set the table with juice glasses and, if you have them, lay out fun plates featuring a holiday motif. If you don't have any, just use your basic white plates. Later on you can head out to the stores for the after-Christmas sales and buy cute holiday plates and any other festive décor at a deep discount to use next year. Use a colorful table runner to bring a little festivity and order to the center of the table. By the way, there's no law that says you can't wrap paper napkins in decorative ribbon, so go ahead and opt for paper instead of cloth to make cleanup even easier. Tie name cards to the napkins with everyone's names or write the names of popular Christmas show characters and let people choose their favorites.

Even if there are no children present, this is a way to unleash the child in all of us. I'll take my seat right at the Cindy Lou Who place, thank you very much, and I'll be humming that Whoville tune throughout breakfast.

On a chilly morning, offer hot chocolate or apple cider with cinnamon sticks. You can also have a saucepan of water and some cinnamon sticks simmering on the stove to fill the house with a beautiful scent.

Food that is easy to make for a crowd is the way to go here. Pancakes, eggs, and some kind of breakfast meat like bacon will do the trick. Recently, I started making chunky pancakes that are loaded with fruit and nuts. They are hearty and have become a crowd-pleaser. Pairing them with thick-sliced bacon has become the go-to combination for me. There is an Amish market near our home in Maryland that sells the freshest applewood bacon. When it is cooking, there is no need for alarm clocks. Everyone in the house seems to wake up and rush right down just from the enticing aromas as it cooks.

ABOVE: Use adorable tree ornaments to decorate the table and make the kids laugh. Other details include colorful curls of ribbon and cute utensils like this candy cane knife.

PARTY PLANNING

Guest Count
8 to 12

The Right Invite
Fry the bacon

Sample Colorway
Red and green

Sample Flower
Red carnations and holly leaves

Musical Vibe
Christmas songs: Harry Connick Jr., Motown, Mariah Carey

Essential Décor Checklist
Casual holiday-themed plates
Flatware
Mugs for coffee and tea
Juice glasses
Platters for the pancakes
Serving bowls for berries
Name cards with a hole punched
Decorative ribbon
Ornaments
White paper napkins
Contrasting place mats
Holiday-inspired table runner
Red carnations and winter greens
Small vases

HEARTY PANCAKES

My recipe uses a packaged pancake mix, which makes preparation quick and easy. I prefer whole wheat batter, but you can choose whatever mix you like. I load these pancakes up with lots of fruit and nuts, making them a hearty family favorite.

Preheat the oven to the lowest setting.

Heat a frying pan or griddle over medium-high heat. Coat the pan with the butter.

Combine the pancake mix, milk, oil, bananas, apple, blueberries, and pecans in a large bowl and stir until any lumps of flour disappear. Pour just under ¼ cup of batter into the pan for each pancake. Cook until you see little bubbles appear and the underside is golden brown. Flip the pancake and cook until it's golden brown underneath. Transfer to a plate and keep warm in the oven until all the pancakes are cooked. Repeat with the remaining batter.

Serves 8

¼ cup (½ stick) butter

2 cups pancake mix

½ cup milk

2 tablespoons vegetable oil

2 overripe bananas, cut into ⅓-inch pieces

½ Gala or Fuji apple, cut into ¼-inch pieces

½ cup blueberries

⅓ cup chopped pecans

GAME DAY PARTY

With the exception of a cute veggie platter, game day is not an occasion for healthy eating. From sliders to chicken wings, fun foods rule the day.

Create an area on your kitchen table, buffet credenza, or kitchen countertop where people can access all the goodies. Placing your team's paraphernalia on the tabletop is a fun way to build the excitement.

Although it's easier when everyone is cheering for the same team, it's okay to mix it up. My family is a combination of New Orleans Saints, Houston Texans, and Washington Commanders fans, so I make sure each team is represented.

Either way, this party is about more than who's playing; it's about the camaraderie among the attendees. When I'm at a party for a team that I'm not a big fan of, I'm still happy for my friends if their team wins and disappointed for them if they lose. 'Cuz here's the thing: How many opportunities do we have in life to scream at people? You can actually yell at the people on the TV screen and no one will yell back at you. Even if you couldn't care less about who wins or loses, it's a great chance to get your frustrations out and then laugh about it.

A successful spread for game day is one that allows guests to move freely about the offerings. Large bowls and platters make it easy for attendees to load up their plates with whatever their heart desires. Feel free to take out your slow cooker and use it to make and serve your best homemade chili or delicious meatballs. It's always nice to offer one tasty dish from scratch that wins the day. For everything else, order your favorite carryout eats at least a week ahead. Set up your table or countertop in advance and simply transfer the food from the carryout containers to serving dishes. It's nice to provide a bowl of wet wipes so guests can clean sticky fingers.

If you have the space, set up two somewhat separate areas with a TV in each—one on mute for the conversationalists who you know will absolutely talk throughout the game. This one is best located nearest the food. Hard-core fans, who need to see the most important plays of the game, can watch the game on the other TV, away from the talkers, so they can focus on who's winning (or not).

Apple Chicken Sausage Sliders

GAME

PARTY PLANNING

Guest Count
6 to 25

The Right Invite
Phone your friends

Sample Colorway
Team colors—I use the Saints' black and gold

Sample Flower
Fuji Football Mums

Musical Vibe
Combat ready: Queen, "We Will Rock You," "Another One Bites the Dust," and "We Are the Champions"; Survivor, "Eye of the Tiger"; DJ Khaled, "All I Do Is Win"

Essential Décor Checklist
Slow cooker
Sturdy paper or other casual appetizer-size plates
Serving dishes in varying heights
Bowls for chili
Utensil organizer
Mini tin buckets for popcorn
Spoons
Team insignia cups
Fun signage
Napkins
Wet wipe packets, for sticky fingers
Serving platters
Ice cooler or bucket for drinks
Team decorations

ABOVE: The details here are all about fun with football-shaped place cards, little buckets for popcorn, and chicken wings. Lots of chicken wings.

Toasted
Mac : Cheese

~ on the menu ~

SMOKY TURKEY CHILI

Chili is a great choice for a crowd at a casual party. All you need to add are a bunch of finger-friendly appetizers, and you'll be good to go. Everybody can serve themselves, so you can watch the game too.

Heat the olive oil in a large pot or Dutch oven over medium heat. Add the turkey and sauté, making sure to break up the meat with a fork, until cooked through, about 20 minutes.

Add the onions, peppers, and garlic and continue to sauté until the veggies are slightly soft, another 5 to 10 minutes.

Add the chili powder, oregano, and Creole seasoning and stir well. Cook, stirring occasionally, for 5 minutes.

Stir in the beans, V8 juice, chopped tomatoes with their juices, and chicken broth and simmer for 30 minutes. Taste and add salt or more seasonings, as needed. Simmer, stirring occasionally, for another 15 minutes.

Transfer to a large slow cooker and continue to cook on low for at least 1 hour.

Serve the chili from the slow cooker, with the optional toppings on the side.

Serves 10 to 14

¼ cup olive oil

3 pounds ground turkey

3 large Vidalia or yellow onions, chopped

1½ large green peppers, seeded and chopped

⅓ cup minced garlic

¾ cup chili powder

1 teaspoon dried oregano

1 teaspoon Tony Chachere's Original Creole Seasoning

1 (16-ounce) can dark kidney beans, drained and rinsed

3 (14-ounce) cans V8 vegetable juice

1 (28-ounce) can chopped tomatoes, with their juices

2 cups chicken broth

1 teaspoon salt

OPTIONAL TOPPINGS
Shredded Cheddar cheese
Sour cream
Chopped scallions

any season

No matter the time of year, it is always appropriate and sometimes critically necessary to engage in a small gathering. There is no correct season for it. These beautiful moments can be planned out meticulously or executed on a whim with no advance planning. Winter, spring, summer, or fall, just be sure to make them happen. Your soul will thank you.

PARTY
FOR ONE

During the winter, my family and I often invite friends over for gumbo, which has to be one of the most supernatural comfort foods ever created. I most often make gumbo with my mother, whose mere presence while we're cooking seems to make the dish even more tasty. Maybe she sprinkles a little extra love in the pot when I'm not watching, but there is no denying that a bowl of that liquid magic is sure to remove any chill in the air and soothe the soul at the same time. After I serve the gumbo and guests leave, I portion the remainder into small containers and freeze it for later, which brings me to the party for one.

I think the most important and rejuvenating gatherings are when I host one for me. As a business owner and mom, I feel like I am always in motion. Even if I'm not physically moving around from my office to construction sites, it seems that my brain is always processing creative ideas and tiny details.

These fast paced times in which we all live can leave us stressed and overstimulated, so I periodically pause to recalibrate and recharge my battery by being still and alone with myself. In these quiet moments, I often pray, meditate, drink a cup of tea, and present myself with a soothing meal. These are the precious still moments when I receive direction and hear messages from the Divine. I also am in a space of gratitude as I consider all of my blessings.

To create your own party for one, make a run to the grocery store or farmers' market to find a small bouquet of flowers that speaks to you. Then, defrost and warm up or order in one of your favorite foods. This is not a time to stress out making a laborious meal in the kitchen. However, if cooking small meals gives you a sense of peace, you can do that too. Otherwise, forego the additional work. Set a place with your favorite dishes, the ones that bring you joy whenever you see them. I have a soup and saucer set from Vietri's Lastra collection that I love and use just for this.

Some of the most life-altering ideas have come to me during these moments, so I make sure that I have a notebook and pen nearby to write down important thoughts. And since I'm in the space of gratitude, I also keep some thank-you notes on the table just in case the spirit moves me to express my appreciation to someone who comes to mind.

No matter how you decide to create your party for one, I highly recommend that you do it monthly or at least seasonally to remind yourself of your own value and that you are worthy of the best things this world has to offer.

BELOW: Set a place for yourself with your favorite china and have a writing utensil and notebook close by. And don't forget to treat yourself to your favorite bouquet of flowers.

PARTY PLANNING

Guest Count
1 (of course)

The Right Invite
Schedule this on your calendar as you would any important meeting

Sample Colorway
Whatever makes you happy

Sample Flower
Any small bouquet that brings you joy

Musical Vibe
Soft instrumental music or no music at all

Essential Décor Checklist
Small bouquet of flowers
Pretty vase for the flowers
Place mat
Cloth napkin
Flatware
Your favorite china
Your favorite glass or mug
Notebook and pen for writing your thoughts
Thank-you notes

MOMMY'S GUMBO

I usually make gumbo for a group of guests and then freeze smaller portions to enjoy later. My mother is known for this recipe and she passed it on to me, so when I need a little lift, indulging in this dish makes me feel like I'm infused with love. A roux is a combination of flour cooked with oil and requires a little patience to get it to the deep dark color that gives gumbo its signature flavor.

Combine the oil and flour in a large glass bowl or microwave-safe measuring cup. Heat in the microwave for 2 minutes. Stir and return to the microwave for 1 minute. Stir and keep repeating this process until the roux mixture reaches the desired color of chocolate brown. Don't overcook. Set aside.

Separate the chicken wing sections by clipping off the wing tips and then cutting the wing into two pieces. Combine the wing tips with the water in a large pot over medium-high heat. Bring to a boil and cook, stirring often, for 30 minutes. Strain the broth into a bowl and discard the solids.

Preheat the oven to 400°F. Line baking sheets with aluminum foil and coat with cooking spray.

Season the remaining meaty wing sections with Creole seasoning and arrange them on the baking sheets. Bake for 15 minutes.

Increase the oven temperature to 450°F. Flip the wing sections and continue to bake for 30 minutes more. Set aside. (You may opt to fry the chicken instead.)

Transfer the roux to a large pot while it is still fairly hot and set over medium heat. Add the chopped onions, garlic, scallions, and parsley and cook, stirring often, until the vegetables are wilted, 5 to 10 minutes.

Add the okra, reserved chicken broth, cooked chicken wings, andouille sausage, and smoked sausage. Fill the pot three-fourths full with water or more chicken broth (if using). Cook, stirring occasionally, for 45 minutes.

Add the shrimp and crabs and simmer for another 30 minutes.

Season well with Creole seasoning and filé powder, to taste, and simmer, stirring occasionally, for 45 minutes.

Serve over cooked rice and garnish with chopped scallions and chopped parsley (if using).

Serves 12 to 15

1 cup oil

1 cup all-purpose flour

5 pounds chicken wings

1 gallon water

Cooking spray

Tony Chachere's Original Creole Seasoning

3 onions, chopped

4 garlic cloves, chopped

1 bunch scallions, chopped, some reserved for optional garnish

1 bunch parsley, chopped, some reserved for optional garnish

2 pounds frozen sliced okra

1 pound andouille sausage, cut in half lengthwise and then sliced

3 pounds smoked Creole sausage, sliced

Chicken broth (optional)

3 pounds peeled and deveined medium shrimp

3 gumbo crabs (optional)

Filé powder

Cooked rice

ESSENTIAL COMPONENTS

With just a few simple items, including flowers, candles, and beautiful place settings, your table-top can look spectacular.

FLOWERS

There is nothing like flowers to bring immediate cheer to a tabletop. Their mere presence adds vibrance, color, and life to any event. Fresh flowers are so pleasing that it is as if they are there specifically to greet and welcome guests when they enter the room. And with so many varieties, the type of flower you choose can complement the intended atmosphere or theme of your gathering.

Although an elaborately arranged bouquet can become the star of the show, and the most amazing ones always take my breath away, I also recognize that there are times when practicality and simplicity are necessary. The most stellar arrangements can be quite costly, and if the budget or the occasion doesn't call for it, taking a shortcut is perfectly fine.

On that note, it is absolutely acceptable to purchase grocery store flowers, if they are in good condition. I say get them where you can, especially when time doesn't allow. The key is to be selective about picking the freshest that are available. My team and I have a spectacular floral supplier near our office that we faithfully use as a resource for photo shoots and installations. However, on occasion, we have also created gorgeous photos of designed spaces by incorporating flowers we found at the grocery store as well as those from the farmers' market. In the end, it's all about how you present them.

That being said, when time and budget allow, I do advocate supporting local florists who have a sense of artistry and provide a wonderful service that is well worth the cost. Whichever way you go, flowers are an essential addition to any tabletop.

Here is an imagery guide to some popular types you may want to consider.

Ranunculus

Snapdragons

Tulips

Alstroemeria

Peonies

Sunflowers

Calla Lillies

Gerbera Daisies

Carnations

Rose

Fuji Mums

Gladiolas

ESSENTIAL PLANNING

There are a few tips and tricks I take advantage of when I'm planning an event that make things easier for me and keeps the focus on my guests.

Ask a Friend We are all so busy with the requirements and tasks of our day-to-day lives that hosting a gathering can sometimes seem overwhelming. This is why it's so important—and perfectly acceptable—to enlist help where you can get it.

Just because a gathering is being hosted at your home doesn't mean that you can't ask for help. Most often, friends are happy to contribute in some way. Ask them to support you by bringing a dish, drinks, or flowers. You can also ask them to help you set up the décor prior to the event. Keep your friends' strengths in mind when assigning tasks. Some will be great at baking, selecting wines, or arranging flowers, while others might have lovely handwriting and can help with the place cards. Whatever you do, don't allow the friend you know is notoriously late to bring anything that has to be served early. Let them bring dessert.

Friends can also lend you serving bowls and platters, serving utensils, or even additional mix-and-match glassware if you have the need but don't want to go out and buy them for one party.

Personalize In my work as an interior designer, I've become known for my ability to personalize spaces and make them memorable. For me, it comes down to identifying what it is that makes each person or brand special and then translating that into design.

If there is one element (or successful strategy) that I would cite as most impactful, it is pinpointing how to make guests feel like they are valued. That might be through writing out name cards, making a special dish someone loves, being sure to spend at least a few minutes with each guest, or texting each one personally afterward to let them know how much you appreciated them coming. These are all ways to make people feel as if they are seen and cared about. And a little care can go a long way and make your event memorable.

Mix and Match If you're expecting more guests than you have place settings for, that's fine. Most people don't have place settings for twenty-four. Go ahead mix and match them. Alternate every other place setting and use a variety of glasses, and it will look artful and intentional. For some uniformity, place a flower on each plate or tucked into a napkin. And as I mentioned earlier, you can also consider borrowing from a friend.

Colorful Ribbon Channel whatever the season is with a piece of ribbon in the color that is synonymous with the time of year. Cut 10- to 12-inch lengths of the ribbon at an angle and tie each one around a napkin. It will make even paper napkins look elevated. Try cutting ribbon in 8-inch lengths and tying them around the stems of wineglasses.

Beautiful! Plus, ribbon is inexpensive and reusable in many cases, so you can keep a variety of colors on hand in a box or large envelope and you're ready to go.

Basic Décor In the images in this book, you'll notice that some items have been reused for multiple occasions. This is the way it is in real life. Most people don't have the budgets or storage capacity to use completely new table elements for every party or gathering they host—especially if they entertain a lot. By changing the colorways and varying other elements such as the types of flowers you use in each gathering, you can reuse table décor successfully while still presenting unique and striking tablescapes every time you host a gathering.

My hope is that you can reuse much of what you already have. If you begin your supply by stocking classic white plates, decent wineglasses, and a crisp white tablecloth, you have the foundation for a great tabletop. These basics will convey the message that the event is special. Almost anything you add would work well with these basics.

Statement Pieces When I design spaces, I try to incorporate one to three memorable "statement" pieces to make a room special. Cute or unique décor items, like decorative place card holders, brightly colored glasses, or a pair of antique salt and pepper shakers can add interest to a tabletop. Whatever you choose, it should be eye-catching or beautiful or spark some sort of conversation.

Just One Thing When creating a lovely gathering, it's not a requirement that everything is created and executed by you. It is perfectly okay to create or rely on one exceptional thing. For example, you can cater your entire occasion and complement it with one dish that you are exceptional at making. Be it your iconic chili, your yummy casserole, or your delightful dessert, you can make your mark with your one uber-memorable dish.

Or maybe your one thing is an ingredient. As you may notice, I use Tony's seasoning a lot in my recipes, and

I do this for good reason. I consider myself a decent cook, but there is one thing that always takes my cooking up a notch, and that is Tony's seasoning. It has some magical combination of ingredients that seem to give a boost to almost any dish. There is even a low-salt version available now for those who need to be health conscious. Honestly, it's available at most grocery stores, so I suggest you try some. For a backup, I rely on my connection to Maryland and use Old Bay Seasoning, which is just perfection with almost any seafood item.

Or maybe your one thing is cute party gifts or swag bags. One of my clients is known to always have cocktail napkins with the most entertaining illustrations or sayings. It has become something her guests look forward to when she is hosting. What is your one thing?

Cater It With all of the responsibilities that load us down on a daily basis, we have to find shortcuts and other ways to reduce stress whenever possible. To that end, there is no shame in the game of having a gathering catered. If you're someone who gets overwhelmed at the mere thought of entertaining, catering may be the exact solution to quell your anxiety and deliver to you and your guests a tasty menu that you escaped preparing.

Then you can focus your energy on the décor and arrange it such that your gathering has some personality. Simply transfer the food into attractive serving dishes if you can before guests arrive.

ESSENTIAL TIPS
AND TIME-SAVERS

Here are a few recommendations on how you can level up a meal or save time and simultaneously be kind to the environment.

UPCYCLE

Saving glass and ceramic yogurt containers and iced tea bottles and repurposing them for flowers or snacks is a great way to take an environmentally friendly approach and also save a little money by avoiding purchasing new containers.

Store away place cards with the names of guests you invite often. Then you can use them over and over.

Many of the items for each occasion in this book are reused in different ways for each gathering. Ramekins, for example, can be used for individualized desserts or mini casseroles, like macaroni and cheese. They are also perfect for serving snacks or to serve toppings for dishes.

TOP IT

In my humble opinion, there is a no-fail time-saving strategy to take a recipe from everyday ho-hum to impressive and fabulous and it requires very little effort, but its impact is huge. Just top it. Level up a standard meal by topping it with a handful of an ingredient, which will give the dish a one-two punch of colorful excitement and flavor. Here are three ingredients I keep on hand to quickly jazz up a recipe.

Berries The visual power of vibrant, colorful berries is incredible. Any basic dessert, homemade or store-bought, can be elevated by topping it with a few colorful berries. A scattering of berries over vanilla ice cream will make this basic dessert seem much more special with very little effort.

Use berries to top yogurt, ice cream, cupcakes, or a slice of Costco pound cake (which, by the way, is very tasty). Dropping one or two raspberries in a glass of Champagne adds festivity and fun to almost any gathering.

Bacon What is it about savory bacon that is so unbelievably mesmerizing? Who knows, and it doesn't matter, because when you add just a little bit of crumbled bacon to a dish, everyone will love it.

Since it is such a fan favorite, I use it often. I broil it in the oven until it's crisp. Then I hammer it into bits with a wooden mallet (which is quite satisfying). Sometimes I sprinkle the bacon directly on a dish and other times I might place it in a cute bowl in front of the dish so guests can spoon their ideal portion on top. This is the best approach if you're unsure if vegetarians are attending your gathering.

Sprinkle it on mac and cheese, green salads, potato salad, deviled eggs, and more. The sky's the limit. Your guests will thank you.

Bread Crumbs Hansel and Gretel really knew what they were doing when they relied on bread crumbs to lead the way. This essential topping has been the final ingredient for me to complete dishes for a very long time.

Almost any casserole can benefit from a sprinkling of bread crumbs and a few additional minutes in the oven, resulting in a beautifully toasted top. They are a mainstay for topping mac and cheese, of course, but they are wonderful on other dishes as well, including stuffed bell peppers, green bean casserole, broccoli and cheese gratin, baked chicken and rice, and pasta casserole.

If your bread crumb toppings are not browned enough after your dish has finished baking, set your oven to a low broil and let them broil for 2 to 3 minutes, until they reach a lovely golden brown. Then serve it immediately and receive oohs and aahs from your guests.

PARTY CHECKLIST

This list may help you organize your next gathering.

- ☐ Candles
- ☐ Candleholder(s)
- ☐ Cups (optional)
- ☐ Dinnerware
- ☐ Flatware
- ☐ Flowers or foliage
- ☐ Glasses
- ☐ Invitations
- ☐ Name cards
- ☐ Name card holders

- ☐ Napkins
- ☐ Napkin rings (optional)
- ☐ Objet d'art
- ☐ Place mats or chargers (optional)
- ☐ Playlist and speaker
- ☐ Ribbon
- ☐ Serving dishes (optional)
- ☐ Serving utensils
- ☐ Tablecloth
- ☐ Vase

Additional Items for a Buffet

- ☐ Hand sanitizer
- ☐ Signage
- ☐ Slow cooker or chafing dishes
- ☐ Utensil caddy

SAMPLE TIMELINE

Planning a party can feel overwhelming sometimes, but it doesn't have to. This is a good timeline to follow for formal or semiformal gatherings, which have more components and take longer to plan. For super casual gatherings, planning things a week ahead should give you plenty of time.

4 Weeks Ahead

☐ Determine what kind of event you're having (the number of guests, the atmosphere, what kind of feeling you want the guests to leave with).

☐ Send out invitations (call, mail, text, email). If you know that most of your guests are super busy, opt for a save-the-date notice at least six to eight weeks in advance.

☐ Decide what will be on the menu.

☐ Request help. If you feel like you could use a little support, there's no shame in the game of asking good friends to bring a dish. Typically, this would be a vegetable, side dish, or dessert that complements the main course.

2 Weeks Ahead

☐ Decide what you will use to serve guests and make sure you have all the components necessary. If you're missing anything, you'll have time to place a quick online order or run to your favorite home store to fill in any gaps.

☐ If you decide to use a caterer, this is the time to place your order. If you have a large order for a popular caterer, you'll want to take care of this many weeks, if not months, in advance.

1 to 2 Weeks Ahead

☐ If you decide to use a florist, this is the time to place an order for fresh flowers.

☐ Decide on and set up your playlist.

1 Week Ahead

☐ Thoroughly clean the spaces that your guests will be in.

☐ Orient your furniture as you want it to appear for the gathering.

☐ Make a list of items you'll need to pick up from the grocery store. Go ahead and purchase nonperishables at this time. That way, you'll have less to do closer to the event.

☐ Decide what you're going to wear.

2 to 3 Days Ahead

☐ Stage and decorate any serving surfaces (tabletop, countertops, buffets) as you would like them to appear for the gathering. Include place cards, napkins, and everything as it will appear on the day of. Cover the plates, serving bowls, and flatware with sheets or towels so they won't collect dust.

2 Days Ahead

- [ ] Purchase any remaining perishable grocery items.

The Day Before

- [ ] Prep the food. Cut veggies and meat for recipes and place them in bowls in the refrigerator so you'll just have to combine them the following day.

- [ ] Pick up flowers and place them in the vases you will use with ice cubes in the water to keep them fresh. Be sure to cut the stems at an angle before placing them in vases or pitchers, which will help them last longer.

The Splendid Day Of

AT LEAST 4 TO 6 HOURS AHEAD

- [ ] Begin cooking. You can assemble everything for dishes early and place them in the refrigerator until it's time for them to go in the oven. For example, you can layer all the ingredients for a casserole ahead and place it in the oven 90 minutes before guests arrive. Let it remain in the oven at a low temperature, and it should be hot and ready to go when it's time to eat.

2 HOURS AHEAD

- [ ] Remove the sheets and towels from the serving surfaces (tabletops, countertops, and buffets). Check the place cards to make sure they are in their appropriate locations.

- [ ] Place vases of flowers in the appropriate locations. Add a few ice cubes to the water, if necessary.

- [ ] If you are using a caterer, have them deliver food 1½ to 2 hours ahead so you have time to transfer them to appropriate serving dishes.

90 MINUTES AHEAD

- [ ] Get dressed. The worst is when a guest confuses the time, shows up early, and you're still in your workout clothes.

30 TO 60 MINUTES AHEAD

- [ ] If you are cooking, plan to have all of your dishes complete. For hot items, keep them in the oven on warm or in a warming drawer until ready to serve.

15 TO 30 MINUTES AHEAD

- [ ] Place snacks out for guests to nosh on before the meal. Make sure drinks are ready to serve. This will relieve your stress. Just in case you or someone else is running late, hungry guests will have something to nibble on while they wait.

- [ ] Start up your playlist.

- [ ] Light the candles.

SHOWTIME

- [ ] Greet your guests with cheer.

BRING THE JOY

In the end, the fact is that the most beautiful tabletop doesn't have a shot at creating a successful event or gathering unless the spirit in the atmosphere is genuine and positive. Joy is the magic ingredient that brings groups of people together and sets the stage for an evening (or brunch, or tea party, or luncheon) that everyone will remember.

So even if your cupboard has only some empty glasses, a few plates, and a bag of chips, fill the glasses with water, dump those chips on the plates, and invite some folks over to share it. Top all of that off with your positive spirit and cheer, and you have the makings of a meaningful gathering.

With Love, Lorna

SOURCES AND CREDITS

SOURCES

Backyard Barbeque
Pages 112 to 123

TABLETOP
Green pitcher and glasses. *Max Studio Home.*
Flatware. *Bamboo Utensils.*
Bamboo Chargers/Plates. *Bambu Store.*
Mini buckets, placards, and tablecloth. *Amazon.*
Salad bowl set. *Prodyne.*

A Blessed Thanksgiving Feast
Pages 150 to 161

TABLETOP
Flatware. *Gorham.*
Candleholders. *Anthropologie.*
Covered dish. *Blue Harbor.*
Aubergine glasses. *Anthropologie.*
Breadbasket. *Lanzarin Ceramiche.*
Hollyhocks and mums. *Potomac Floral Wholesale.*

INTERIOR DESIGN
LORNA GROSS Interior Design

Chic Cocktail Party
Pages 162 to 175

APPETIZER HIGH TOP
Curate stand. *Sur la Table.*
Custom quartz tray. *Cambria.*
Cocktail napkins. *Slant Collections.*

COCKTAIL TABLE
Multi-colored cocktail glasses. *Anthropologie.*
Ice buckets. *Mikasa.*
Decanter. *Baccarat.*
Brass candleholders. *Anthropologie.*

INTERIOR DESIGN
LORNA GROSS Interior Design

Cozy Afternoon Tea
Pages 126 to 135

TABLETOP
Accent plates. *Mikasa.*
Antique tea set. *Limoges (France).*
Petite blue vases. *Joanna Gaines for Target.*
Curate tiered tray stand. *Sur La Table.*

INTERIOR DESIGN
LORNA GROSS Interior Design

Delightfully Casual Dinner
Pages 62 to 71

TABLETOP
Casserole dish. *Vietri thru Bloomingdales.*
Table runner. *Anthropologie.*
Green glasses. *Anthropologie.*
Salt and pepper dispensers. *Blue Pheasant to the trade.*
Glass serving spoons. *Ichendorf Milano.*
Flatware. *Rachel Ashwell.*
Dinner Plates. *Target.*

Formal Christmas Dinner
Pages 190 to 203

TABLETOP
Gold edged charger plates. *Vietri.*
Accent plates. *Wedgewood.*
Name card holders. *Corbell Silver.*
Gold-dotted napkins. *All Cotton and Linen.*
Bejeweled plate ornaments. *Leila's Linens.*
Centerpiece bowl. *John Richard.*

INTERIOR DESIGN
LORNA GROSS Interior Design

Friendsgiving Outdoor Dinner
Pages 136 to 149

TABLETOP
Accent plates. *Anthropologie.*
Napkin rings. *The Old Town Shop, Alexandria, VA.*
Name card holders. *Pottery Barn.*
Mums and foliage. *Potomac Floral Wholesale.*

Frosty Holiday Dinner
Pages 178 to 189

TABLETOP
Napkin rings. *Kim Seybert.*
Dinnerware. *Tabletop Gallery.*
Silver edged napkins. *Tahari Home.*
Silver twigs. *Crate and Barrel.*
Flatware and holiday décor. *HomeGoods.*

INTERIOR DESIGN
LORNA GROSS Interior Design

Game Day Party
Pages 216 to 227

TABLETOP
Chip bowl. *Crate & Barrel.*
Ice bucket. *Amazon.*

COUNTERTOP
Game day décor. *Oriental Trading.*
Popcorn Tins. *Amazon.*
Utensil caddy and serving dishes. *HomeGoods.*
Platters. *IKEA.*
Football mums and Eucalyptus: Potomac Floral Wholesale.

Lazy Summer Breakfast
Pages 102 to 111

TABLETOP
Linen table runner. *Mark & Graham.*
Wooden serving platforms and pitcher. *HomeGoods.*
Ranunculus. *Potomac Floral Wholesale.*

COUNTERTOP
Mini quiche ramekins. *Cuire.*
Foliage and Gerbera daisies. *Potomac Floral Wholesale.*
Caddy and cake stand. *HomeGoods.*

INTERIOR DESIGN
LORNA GROSS Interior Design

Lush Garden Luncheon
Pages 74 to 89

TABLETOP
Goblets. *Bormioli Rocco.*
Table throw. *Lily Pulitzer.*
Dessert ramekins. *Cuire.*
Tablecloth. *Quality Living.*
Foliage and florals. *Potomac Floral Wholesale.*

EXTERIOR DESIGN
LORNA GROSS Interior Design

Moody Formal Dinner
Pages 36 to 49

TABLETOP
Dinnerware. *Vera Wang for Wedgewood.*
Charcoal glasses. *La Rochere.*

Candleholders. *Anthropologie.*
Metallic place mats. *Kim Seybert.*
Flatware. *Gorham.*
Salt and pepper dispensers. *Jonathan Adler.*
Crystal wineglasses. *Mikasa.*

CREDENZA
Black glass decanter. *Curated Kravet.*
Vintage vase. *1st Dibs.*

INTERIOR DESIGN
LORNA GROSS Interior Design

Party For One

TABLETOP
Soup and salad dinnerware. *Vietri—Nieman Marcus.*
and *Crème de la Crème, Virginia.*

INTERIOR DESIGN
LORNA GROSS Interior Design

Post-Christmas Breakfast

TABLETOP
Holiday dinnerware and serving bowl. *Target.*
Holiday ribbon. *Decor Lane.*
Table runner. *Cynthia Rowley.*

INTERIOR DESIGN
LORNA GROSS Interior Design

Sunday Brunch

TABLETOP
Blush goblets. *Godinger.*
Hollyhock florals. *Potomac Floral Wholesale.*
Linen table runner. *Mark and Graham.*
Butter dish. *Palate and Plate.*
Bread basket. *Lanzarin Ceramiche.*

BUFFET
Blush water glasses. *Bormioli Rocco.*

INTERIOR DESIGN
LORNA GROSS Interior Design

Welcome Spring Buffet Dinner

COUNTERTOP
Custom quartz tray. *Cambria.*
Linen table runner. *Mark & Graham.*
Calla lilies. *Potomac Floral Wholesale.*

Y'all Come! Seafood Feast

TABLETOP
Platter. *Rachel Roy.*
Mason jars, crab crackers and tools, butcher paper roll. *Amazon.*
Wooden mallets. *Southern Homewares.*
Red and white tablecloth. *Homedecr.*
Lanterns. *Kate Aspen.*

CREDITS

Cover and Primary Photography: *Robert Radifera*
Additional Photography: *Keyanna Bowen—pages 11, 50, 53-56, 60-61, 72-73, 102, 104-106, 110-111, 72-73, 102, 104-106, 110-111, 124-126, 129-130, 134-135, 246*

Assistant Shoot Stylist: *Lillie Honiberg*
Shoot Team Members: *Hillarie Anderson, Autumn Bryant, Jennifer Grant, Debbie Haryono, Teri Mazariegos, Campbell Shepherdson, Marin Shutty, Diana Vallejos, Lauren Gaston,* and *Jordan Miller.*
Hair Stylist: *Blake Holloway*

ACKNOWLEDGMENTS

To My Belief Posse, Andrea, Renata, Sharon, Randie, and Rosie, you were steadfast believers when this venture was a mere idea. Thank you for your enthusiastic encouragement and for continuing to breathe faith into me and motivate me to glow up. You poured fuel in my tank when I didn't think I had any left.

To my mother, the person who taught me how to set a beautiful table. You were the first believer who knew her daughter was an outlier and a maverick, and you intentionally gave me permission and creative space to blaze trails and to become what had not yet been imagined.

To Dom, Celeste, and Lisa, I so appreciate your constant prayers and support. To the sisters of the BOW Collective, thanks for the inspiration.

Thank you to my clients and friends—Penny, Greg, DeDe, Dallas, Emma, Brooks, LB, Pierson, Pepper, Hope, David, A. Scott, Adriana, Marli, and John for your support and for opening up your gorgeous spaces to me.

To Robert and Lillie for your positive energy on those intricate photo shoots. Thank you for helping me create something beautiful despite fatigue, 100-degree days, and rain and trees falling down around us.

Thanks to Leslie Jonath, Amy Treadwell, and the whole team at the Collective Book Studio for your knowledge and wonderful guidance through the process of making this book become a reality. Thank you Bremante' for chiming in on my random questions.

To my incredible Louisiana community, Janet Cloudet, the Washington-Davis family, PJ's Bowie, and Susan Gravely, thank you for instilling in me and reminding me that the essence of human connection and gathering, at its core, is based in beauty, love, and fellowship.

Thank you, God, for your great faithfulness.

Library of Congress Cataloging-in-Publication Data available.
ISBN: 978-1-68555-578-8
Ebook ISBN: 978-1-68555-711-9
Library of Congress Control Number: 2024901405

Printed using Forest Stewardship Council certified stock
from sustainably managed forests.

Manufactured in China.
Design by Suzi Hutsell

1 3 5 7 9 10 8 6 4 2

The Collective Book Studio®
Oakland, California
www.thecollectivebook.studio